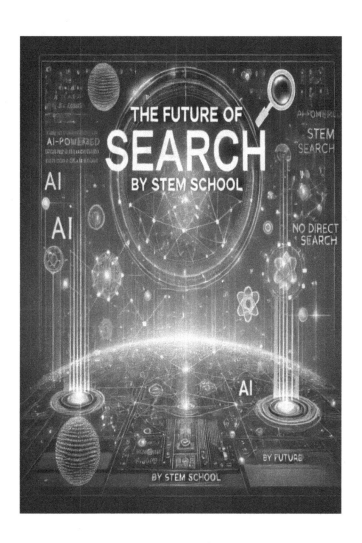

AI and the Future of Search

How Intelligent Algorithms Are Transforming Online Discovery

By

STEM School

This Page Left Intentionally Blank

Contents

Search engines have become an integral part of our digital lives, helping us navigate the vast ocean of online information. However, traditional search engines rely heavily on keyword matching and predefined ranking algorithms, often leading to results that may not fully align with user intent. The rise of artificial intelligence (AI) has transformed this landscape, enabling search engines to provide more relevant, context-aware, and personalized results.

Limitations of Traditional Search Engines

Traditional search engines function primarily through keyword-based indexing and ranking. When a user enters a query, the search engine scans its vast database to retrieve results that match the keywords entered. However, this approach has several limitations

Keyword Dependency Traditional search engines rely on exact keyword matches, which means users must phrase their queries carefully to get relevant results. If a user searches for "best ways to stay fit," the engine might not recognize similar queries like "top fitness strategies" as being equivalent.

Lack of Contextual Understanding Since these engines do not truly "understand" user intent, they might return results that match individual words rather than the overall meaning of the query. For

6

example, searching for "apple nutrition facts" might return results for both the fruit and the technology company if context is not properly considered.

Limited Personalization   Most traditional search engines use general ranking algorithms that do not adapt to individual user preferences. Two different users searching for "best smartphones" might get similar results, even if one is more interested in gaming phones while the other prefers budget-friendly options.

Inability to Handle Complex Queries   Traditional search engines struggle with nuanced, long-form, or conversational queries. Questions like "What are the safest investment options for retirees in 2025?" require an understanding of multiple factors, including financial trends, risk assessment, and user intent.

The Role of AI in Enhancing Search Accuracy

AI-powered search engines overcome these limitations by incorporating advanced technologies such as **natural language processing (NLP)**, **machine learning (ML)**, and **deep learning algorithms**. These technologies enable a shift from keyword-based searches to intent-driven, contextual understanding of user queries.

Natural Language Processing (NLP)

NLP allows search engines to interpret queries more like a human would, understanding not just individual words but their meanings in context. This means users can input more conversational queries, and the engine will still return the most relevant results. For instance, if a user asks, "What are some good places to visit in Paris during winter?" an AI-powered search engine can analyze "Paris," "visit," and "winter" in relation to each other rather than treating them as isolated terms.

Machine Learning (ML) and Continuous Improvement

Machine learning enables search engines to learn from past interactions and improve over time. By analyzing user behavior—such as which search results are clicked, how much time is spent on a page, and whether users refine their queries—AI can optimize future search rankings to deliver better results.

Semantic Search and Context Awareness

Unlike traditional keyword-based search, semantic search considers the meaning behind words. AI models can recognize synonyms, relationships between words, and even user preferences based on past search history. For example, searching for "healthy breakfast options" might return results about oatmeal, smoothies, and protein-packed meals rather than simply pages that contain the exact phrase "healthy breakfast options."

Personalized Search Experience

AI-powered search engines can tailor results based on individual user data, such as search history, location, and preferences. A user searching for "best laptops" may receive different recommendations based on their browsing history—someone interested in gaming will see high-performance laptops, while a student may see budget-friendly options.

Table Comparison of Traditional vs. AI-Powered Search Engines

Feature	Traditional Search Engines	AI-Powered Search Engines
Keyword Dependency	High	Low (understands intent)
Context Awareness	Low	High (interprets meaning)
Personalization	Limited	Highly personalized results
Handling Complex Queries	Struggles with long-form or	Excels at understanding

Feature	Traditional Search Engines	AI-Powered Search Engines
	nuanced queries	context and depth
Learning & Adaptation	Static algorithms	Continuously improves with machine learning

The Future of AI in Search Technology

As AI continues to evolve, search engines will become even more sophisticated. Future advancements may include

Voice and Conversational Search With improvements in voice recognition and NLP, AI-powered search engines will better understand spoken queries, making voice search more accurate and user-friendly.

Multimodal Search AI will enable users to search using a combination of text, images, and even videos. For example, users could upload a picture of a plant and receive results identifying its species along with care instructions.

Deeper Personalization AI will refine personalization further by considering more aspects of user preferences, such as reading habits, previous searches, and even real-time contextual data like current location and time of day.

Ethical AI and Bias Reduction Efforts will be made to ensure AI-powered search engines provide unbiased and fair search results, reducing misinformation and improving information credibility.

AI-powered search engines represent a major leap forward from traditional search methods. By leveraging NLP, ML, and semantic search, these advanced systems provide more accurate, personalized, and intuitive search experiences. As AI technology continues to improve, search engines will become even better at understanding user intent, making information retrieval faster and more relevant than ever before. The integration of AI into search is not just an upgrade—it is a necessity for the future of digital information discovery.

Chapter 1

Evolution of Search Engines

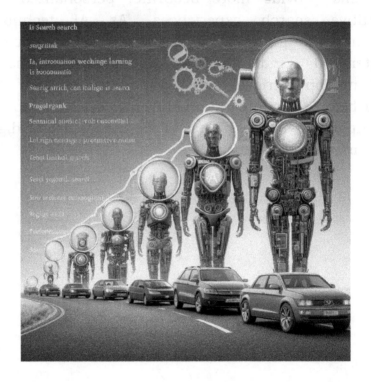

The journey of search engines has been one of continuous evolution, adapting to the growing complexity of the internet and the increasing expectations of users. From their early days of keyword-based search to the modern AI-powered engines that predict and personalize results, search technology has undergone a remarkable transformation. Understanding this evolution is crucial to appreciating the role AI plays in today's search experience.

The Early Days of Search Engines

In the early days of the internet, search engines relied entirely on keyword-based models, where results were retrieved based on exact matches between search queries and indexed content. The two fundamental techniques used were **Boolean search** and **basic keyword matching**.

Boolean search allowed users to refine queries using logical operators such as AND, OR, and NOT. For instance, searching for "apple AND nutrition" would return only pages containing both words, whereas "apple OR nutrition" would return pages containing either term. While effective for structured databases, Boolean search was limited in handling ambiguous or natural language queries.

The first generation of search engines, such as **Archie (1990), Veronica (1992), and Lycos (1994)**, worked by indexing web pages and retrieving results purely based on textual matches. There was no ranking mechanism to prioritize relevant information, making search results overwhelming and inefficient.

As the internet expanded, new algorithms were developed to rank search results based on relevance. One of the most revolutionary advancements came with **PageRank**, developed by Google founders Larry Page and Sergey Brin in 1998.

The Birth of Modern Search Ranking

PageRank introduced the concept of ranking web pages based on their importance, measured by the number and quality of links pointing to them. Instead of merely retrieving pages containing a search term, this algorithm prioritized those that were deemed authoritative.

For example, if a webpage about "healthy diets" had numerous reputable sites linking to it, it would be ranked higher than a page with little to no backlinks, even if both contained the same keywords. PageRank dramatically improved search relevance, laying the foundation for Google's dominance in the search industry.

However, keyword dependency still posed problems. Webmasters could manipulate rankings by stuffing pages with excessive keywords or using deceptive link-building tactics, leading to low-quality search results. This necessitated further advancements in search technology.

The Introduction of Machine Learning and Big Data

As the internet grew, so did the need for more intelligent search engines capable of handling vast amounts of data. Machine learning (ML) and big data analytics began playing a crucial role in refining search results.

One of the first major implementations of ML in search was **Google's RankBrain (2015)**, an AI-driven algorithm designed to understand user intent and improve search accuracy. Unlike static algorithms, RankBrain learned from past queries to interpret new, unseen searches more effectively.

For instance, if a user searched for "best phones for photography," RankBrain would analyze past interactions with similar queries and infer that users were looking for smartphones with high-quality cameras. Instead of simply returning pages containing the phrase "best phones for photography," it ranked results based on user engagement and relevance.

Big data also became a crucial element in improving search performance. Search engines collected massive amounts of user data—such as browsing history, location, and click behavior—to refine results. This data-driven approach led to more **personalized search experiences**, where results were tailored to individual preferences rather than being one-size-fits-all.

The Rise of Semantic Search

One of the most significant shifts in search engine evolution was the transition from **keyword-based search to semantic search**. Semantic search goes beyond literal keyword matching by understanding the meaning behind words and phrases.

For example, a traditional search engine might interpret the query "Apple stock price" as a request for web pages containing those exact words. In contrast, a semantic search engine recognizes that the user is likely looking for real-time stock market data related to Apple Inc. and retrieves relevant financial reports, stock tickers, and news articles.

This leap in search intelligence was made possible by **natural language processing (NLP) and deep learning**. NLP allows search engines to interpret conversational queries, making searches more intuitive.

To illustrate this evolution, consider the following comparison

Feature	Keyword-Based Search	Semantic Search
Focus	Matches exact words	Understands intent and meaning
Example Query	"Best laptop under $1000"	"Which laptop offers the best value under $1000?"
Results	Returns pages with the phrase "best laptop under $1000"	Analyzes reviews, expert opinions, and user preferences to suggest relevant products
Adaptability	Static (fixed algorithms)	Dynamic (continuously learning)

The introduction of **Google's Knowledge Graph (2012)** marked another milestone in semantic search.

Instead of treating search terms as isolated keywords, the Knowledge Graph connected related entities.

For example, searching for "Leonardo da Vinci" not only returned biographical pages but also displayed a knowledge panel summarizing his birth, notable works, and historical impact. This shift allowed search engines to provide **direct answers** rather than just links.

Emergence of Search Personalization and Predictive Search

As AI became more sophisticated, search engines moved towards **personalized and predictive search models**.

Personalized search uses AI to analyze individual preferences, location, and past searches to deliver customized results. If a user frequently searches for **vegan recipes**, their search results for "healthy meal ideas" might prioritize plant-based options. Similarly, someone searching for "football news" in the UK might see results about the **Premier League**, whereas a US user might get **NFL updates**.

Predictive search takes this a step further by anticipating what users want before they finish typing. Google's **Autocomplete** and **Google Discover** are examples of predictive AI in action. Autocomplete suggests queries in real time, while Discover curates content based on user interests, even when they aren't actively searching.

To illustrate the progression from traditional search to AI-driven models, the following timeline highlights key milestones

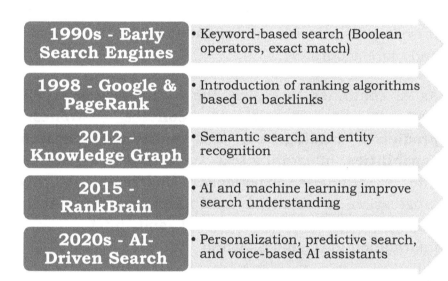

1990s - Early Search Engines	• Keyword-based search (Boolean operators, exact match)
1998 - Google & PageRank	• Introduction of ranking algorithms based on backlinks
2012 - Knowledge Graph	• Semantic search and entity recognition
2015 - RankBrain	• AI and machine learning improve search understanding
2020s - AI-Driven Search	• Personalization, predictive search, and voice-based AI assistants

The evolution of search engines has been shaped by the need for **better relevance, deeper understanding, and greater personalization**. Early keyword-based models laid the groundwork, but they struggled with ambiguity and manipulation. The introduction of ranking algorithms, machine learning, and big data helped refine search results, making them more useful and personalized.

The rise of semantic search marked a significant shift by allowing search engines to understand meaning and context rather than relying on exact keywords. AI-powered algorithms, such as RankBrain and predictive search, have made search engines more intuitive, providing users with the information they need faster and more accurately.

As AI continues to evolve, the future of search will likely involve even greater **context awareness, predictive intelligence, and multimodal search capabilities**, integrating text, voice, and visual search into a seamless experience. Understanding this progression is essential to appreciating how AI is transforming the way we find and interact with information in the digital world.

Chapter 2

Understanding the Core of Search Engines

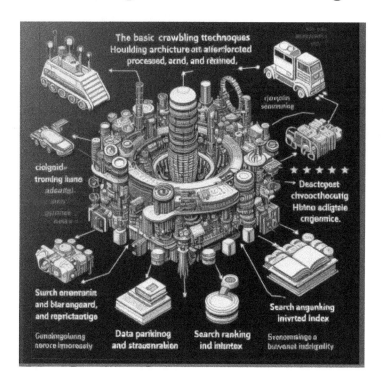

Search engines have transformed the way we access and retrieve information on the internet. Behind the seemingly simple action of typing a query and receiving relevant results lies a sophisticated architecture that processes massive amounts of data in real-time. This chapter explores the fundamental components of search engines, detailing how they collect, process, index, and retrieve data to ensure optimal search performance.

The Architecture of a Search Engine

A search engine operates through a multi-stage process involving **web crawling, data parsing, indexing, and retrieval**. These stages form the backbone of search technology, ensuring that users receive accurate and relevant results. The diagram below illustrates a high-level overview of how search engines function

Each component plays a critical role in determining how search engines understand and rank webpages.

Web Crawling Collecting Data from the Web

Web crawling is the first step in search engine operations. It involves systematically browsing the internet to discover and collect web pages. Search engines deploy **web crawlers**, also known as **spiders** or **bots**, to traverse websites and retrieve content for indexing.

There are two primary strategies for web crawling

Depth-First Crawling (DFS)

This method follows links on a webpage as deeply as possible before backtracking. If a crawler lands on a homepage, it will explore all internal links within that page before moving to other domains. This approach is useful for discovering deeply nested content but may overlook broader site structures.

Breadth-First Crawling (BFS)

In this method, the crawler explores all links on a page before moving deeper into any one section. This ensures comprehensive coverage of different websites and is widely used for general-purpose web indexing.

The effectiveness of a crawler depends on factors such as **crawl budget**, **robots.txt rules**, and **handling dynamic content**. Modern crawlers can parse JavaScript-heavy pages and respect website-specific restrictions.

Basic Web Crawler Using BeautifulSoup & Requests

```
import requests
from bs4 import BeautifulSoup

def simple_crawler(url, depth=1)
    if depth == 0
        return

    try
        response = requests.get(url)
        if response.status_code == 200
            soup = BeautifulSoup(response.text, 'html.parser')
            print(f"Crawled {url}")

            # Extract and follow links
            for link in soup.find_all('a', href=True)
                new_url = link['href']
                if new_url.startswith("http")
                    simple_crawler(new_url, depth-1)
    except Exception as e
        print(f"Failed to crawl {url} {e}")

# Example usage
simple_crawler("https //example.com", depth=2)
```

Data Parsing and Structuring Information

Once a web page is crawled, its content needs to be structured into a readable format. Web pages are often written in **HTML and XML**, requiring parsing techniques to extract relevant data.

HTML Parsing helps identify text content, metadata, and links. Libraries like **BeautifulSoup** and **lxml** can be used to extract page elements such as titles, headings, and body text.

XML Parsing is useful for handling structured data, such as sitemaps and RSS feeds.

Consider a case where we extract the title and all headings from a webpage

```
def extract_content(url)
    response = requests.get(url)
    soup = BeautifulSoup(response.text, 'html.parser')

    title = soup.title.string if soup.title else "No Title"
    headings = [h.text.strip() for h in soup.find_all(['h1', 'h2', 'h3'])]

    return {"title"  title, "headings"  headings}

print(extract_content("https //example.com"))
```

This structured data is then used for indexing, which enables fast and efficient retrieval.

Building and Maintaining an Inverted Index

A search engine's efficiency depends on its ability to retrieve documents quickly. Instead of scanning entire documents for every query, search engines use **inverted indexes**—a data structure that maps keywords to document locations.

What is an Inverted Index?

An inverted index is a mapping from words (tokens) to the documents in which they appear. Consider the following example

Word	Documents
Machine	Doc1, Doc3
Learning	Doc1, Doc2
Python	Doc2, Doc3

If a user searches for "Machine Learning," the engine can quickly retrieve **Doc1 and Doc2** without scanning every document.

Creating a Simple Inverted Index

from collections import defaultdict

```
def build_inverted_index(docs)
    index = defaultdict(set)
    for doc_id, content in docs.items()
        words = content.lower().split()
        for word in words
            index[word].add(doc_id)
    return index

documents = {
    "Doc1"  "Machine learning is a subset of AI",
    "Doc2"  "Python is widely used in AI and machine learning",
    "Doc3"  "Deep learning is part of machine learning"
}

inverted_index = build_inverted_index(documents)
print(inverted_index)
```

This approach ensures that search engines can find relevant documents with minimal computational overhead.

Search Ranking Relevance and Authority

Once a search query is processed, search engines must rank results based on **relevance and authority**. Several ranking factors determine the order in which pages appear

Ranking Factor	Description
TF-IDF (Term Frequency-Inverse Document	Measures keyword importance in a document relative to other

Ranking Factor	Description
Frequency)	documents.
PageRank	Evaluates a page's authority based on inbound links.
User Behavior	Click-through rates (CTR) and dwell time impact rankings.
Semantic Understanding	AI-driven models like BERT analyze query intent.

Modern search engines, such as Google, leverage **machine learning** to continuously refine ranking algorithms, ensuring that results align with user expectations.

Implementing Search Ranking with Elasticsearch

Elasticsearch is a powerful search engine built for handling large-scale indexing and retrieval. The following code demonstrates indexing documents and executing a simple search query

```
from elasticsearch import Elasticsearch

es = Elasticsearch("http //localhost 9200")

# Indexing documents
docs = [
```

```
    {"id"  1, "text"  "Machine learning is transforming AI"},
    {"id"  2, "text"  "Python is a versatile language for AI"},
    {"id"  3, "text"  "Search engines rely on inverted indexing"}
]

for doc in docs
    es.index(index="search_engine", id=doc["id"], body=doc)

# Searching for a term
query = {"query"  {"match"  {"text"  "AI"}}}
results = es.search(index="search_engine", body=query)
print(results)
```

This example showcases how search engines efficiently retrieve and rank relevant documents.

Understanding the architecture of search engines reveals the complexity behind seemingly simple search queries. Web crawlers collect vast amounts of data, which is then parsed, structured, and indexed for efficient retrieval. The introduction of inverted indexing has revolutionized search speed, while advanced ranking algorithms ensure users receive the most relevant results. With AI-driven improvements, search engines are becoming more sophisticated, moving towards **intent-driven, personalized, and context-aware search experiences**. The next chapter will explore how **AI and deep learning models** are further refining search capabilities, enabling even smarter and more human-like interactions in search technology.

Chapter 3

Introduction to AI in Search

The integration of Artificial Intelligence (AI) in search engines has fundamentally transformed the way information is retrieved, making search systems more **intelligent, contextual, and user-centric**. Traditional keyword-based search engines relied heavily on exact word matches, often failing to understand the nuances of user queries. AI introduces advanced techniques such as **Natural Language Processing (NLP), Machine Learning (ML), neural networks, and reinforcement learning**, which allow search engines to interpret intent, rank results based on relevance, and continuously learn from user interactions.

This chapter explores how AI-powered search engines work, covering the essential AI-driven components that enhance search experiences. By the end of this chapter, readers will understand the role of AI in search and gain practical insights into implementing AI models using **TensorFlow and PyTorch**.

Natural Language Processing (NLP

Traditional search engines struggle to understand queries beyond exact keyword matches. AI-powered search engines, however, leverage **Natural Language Processing (NLP) to interpret user intent, recognize synonyms, understand context, and handle ambiguous queries**.

NLP enables search engines to process **human language** in a meaningful way. A simple example is how Google processes the query

📌 **Traditional Search** "best laptops for students" → Matches pages with exact terms "best," "laptops," and "students."

📌 **AI-Powered Search** "best laptops for students" → Understands that "students" may need affordable, lightweight, long-battery-life laptops.

Components of NLP in Search

NLP consists of multiple techniques that improve search understanding

📌 **Tokenization** → Splitting sentences into individual words or phrases.

📌 **Named Entity Recognition (NER)** → Identifying entities like people, locations, or products.

📌 **Part-of-Speech (POS) Tagging** → Understanding the grammatical role of words.

📌 **Word Embeddings** → Mapping words to numerical vectors to understand relationships.

A simple **Python implementation of NLP-based query processing** using **spaCy**

```
import spacy

nlp = spacy.load("en_core_web_sm")

query = "Find the best laptop for college students"
doc = nlp(query)

print("Tokens ", [token.text for token in doc])
print("Entities ", [(ent.text, ent.label_) for ent in doc.ents])
```

Output

```
Tokens ['Find', 'the', 'best', 'laptop', 'for', 'college', 'students']
Entities [('college', 'ORG')]
```

This demonstrates how NLP identifies essential parts of a query to refine search results.

Machine Learning (ML) Models for Ranking

Search ranking is one of the most critical tasks in a search engine. **Machine Learning (ML) models analyze query-document relationships, user behavior, and content quality to rank results dynamically**. Unlike traditional ranking algorithms (such as PageRank), ML-driven ranking models continuously **learn from user clicks, dwell time, and engagement metrics** to improve search quality.

How ML Improves Search Ranking

Traditional Ranking	ML-Based Ranking
Relies on fixed rules (e.g., keyword matching, backlinks)	Learns from user behavior and adapts dynamically
Struggles with complex queries and synonyms	Understands query semantics and intent
Limited personalization	Provides personalized search results based on user preferences

A practical **Python implementation using scikit-learn** to train a basic ranking model

```
from sklearn.feature_extraction.text import TfidfVectorizer
from sklearn.ensemble import RandomForestRegressor

# Sample documents and relevance scores
documents = ["Best budget laptop for students", "Gaming laptop
with high performance", "Lightweight laptop with long battery
life"]
queries = ["laptop for students"]
relevance_scores = [1, 0, 0.8]

vectorizer = TfidfVectorizer()
X = vectorizer.fit_transform(documents)
model = RandomForestRegressor()

model.fit(X.toarray(), relevance_scores)
```

```
query_vector = vectorizer.transform(queries).toarray()
predicted_relevance = model.predict(query_vector)

print("Predicted Relevance ", predicted_relevance)
```

This demonstrates how ML models can rank search results based on relevance.

Neural Networks for Contextual Understanding

Neural networks enable search engines to **grasp context and meaning** rather than just matching keywords. Deep learning models such as **BERT (Bidirectional Encoder Representations from Transformers)** help search engines understand user queries in a **more human-like way**.

For example, consider the query ✦ **"Can you tell me how to bank?"**

- A traditional search engine might return **financial institutions.**
- An AI-powered search engine using BERT understands that "bank" could mean **riverbank** or **financial bank**, depending on context.

Implementing a Neural Search Model Using BERT

```
from transformers import BertTokenizer, TFBertModel
import tensorflow as tf

tokenizer = BertTokenizer.from_pretrained("bert-base-uncased")
model = TFBertModel.from_pretrained("bert-base-uncased")

query = "How to open a bank account?"
tokens = tokenizer(query, return_tensors="tf")
output = model(**tokens)

print("Query            Vector            Representation            ",
output.last_hidden_state.numpy())
```

This technique enables AI-powered search engines to better **understand nuances and context in search queries**.

Reinforcement Learning for Improving Search

Reinforcement Learning (RL) allows search engines to **learn and improve search quality dynamically based on user interactions**. Instead of relying on pre-defined rules, RL-based search engines adjust rankings based on **real-world feedback** from users.

How RL Enhances Search Engines

📌 **Reward Signals** → Click-through rates (CTR), dwell time, and user satisfaction provide feedback.
📌 **Exploration vs. Exploitation** → The model tests new ranking strategies while optimizing proven ones.
📌 **Adaptive Learning** → The search engine refines ranking models over time for better results.

A **simple reinforcement learning example** using PyTorch

```
import torch
import torch.nn as nn
import torch.optim as optim

# Simple RL Model for Search Optimization
class SearchRL(nn.Module)
    def __init__(self)
        super(SearchRL, self).__init__()
        self.fc = nn.Linear(10, 1)

    def forward(self, x)
        return torch.sigmoid(self.fc(x))

model = SearchRL()
optimizer = optim.Adam(model.parameters(), lr=0.01)

# Simulated reward for user interactions
reward = torch.tensor([1.0])
prediction = model(torch.rand(10))

loss = (prediction - reward) ** 2
```

```
loss.backward()
optimizer.step()

print("Updated model weights ", model.fc.weight)
```

By applying **reinforcement learning**, search engines can dynamically **refine rankings based on actual user engagement**, leading to **continuous improvement in search quality**.

AI has revolutionized search engines by introducing **natural language processing, machine learning, neural networks, and reinforcement learning**. These technologies allow search engines to **understand context, improve ranking accuracy, and adapt to user behavior** dynamically. The future of search lies in **self-learning, personalized, and AI-driven models**, which will make search engines smarter, faster, and more human-like. In the next chapter, we will explore **how AI-powered search personalization and predictive search work**, diving deeper into real-world applications and case studies.

Chapter 3

Introduction to AI in Search

The integration of Artificial Intelligence (AI) in search engines has fundamentally transformed the way information is retrieved, making search systems more **intelligent, contextual, and user-centric**. Traditional keyword-based search engines relied heavily on exact word matches, often failing to understand the nuances of user queries. AI introduces advanced techniques such as **Natural Language Processing (NLP), Machine Learning (ML), neural networks, and reinforcement learning**, which allow search engines to interpret intent, rank results based on relevance, and continuously learn from user interactions.

This chapter explores how AI-powered search engines work, covering the essential AI-driven components that enhance search experiences. By the end of this chapter, readers will understand the role of AI in search and gain practical insights into implementing AI models using **TensorFlow and PyTorch**.

Natural Language Processing (NLP) for User Queries

Traditional search engines struggle to understand queries beyond exact keyword matches. AI-powered search engines, however, leverage **Natural Language Processing (NLP)** to **interpret user intent, recognize synonyms, understand context, and handle ambiguous queries**.

NLP enables search engines to process **human language** in a meaningful way. A simple example is how Google processes the query

✦ **Traditional Search** "best laptops for students" → Matches pages with exact terms "best," "laptops," and "students."

✦ **AI-Powered Search** "best laptops for students" → Understands that "students" may need affordable, lightweight, long-battery-life laptops.

Components of NLP in Search

NLP consists of multiple techniques that improve search understanding

✦ **Tokenization** → Splitting sentences into individual words or phrases.

✦ **Named Entity Recognition (NER)** → Identifying entities like people, locations, or products.

✦ **Part-of-Speech (POS) Tagging** → Understanding the grammatical role of words.

✦ **Word Embeddings** → Mapping words to numerical vectors to understand relationships.

A simple **Python implementation of NLP-based query processing** using **spaCy**

```
import spacy
nlp = spacy.load("en_core_web_sm")

query = "Find the best laptop for college students"
doc = nlp(query)

print("Tokens ", [token.text for token in doc])
print("Entities ", [(ent.text, ent.label_) for ent in doc.ents])
```

Output

Tokens ['Find', 'the', 'best', 'laptop', 'for', 'college', 'students']
Entities [('college', 'ORG')]

This demonstrates how NLP identifies essential parts of a query to refine search results.

Machine Learning (ML) Models

Search ranking is one of the most critical tasks in a search engine. **Machine Learning (ML) models analyze query-document relationships, user behavior, and content quality to rank results dynamically**. Unlike traditional ranking algorithms (such as PageRank), ML-driven ranking models continuously **learn from user clicks, dwell time, and engagement metrics** to improve search quality.

How ML Improves Search Ranking

Traditional Ranking	ML-Based Ranking
Relies on fixed rules (e.g., keyword matching, backlinks)	Learns from user behavior and adapts dynamically
Struggles with complex queries and synonyms	Understands query semantics and intent
Limited personalization	Provides personalized search results based on user preferences

A practical **Python implementation using scikit-learn** to train a basic ranking model

```
from sklearn.feature_extraction.text import TfidfVectorizer
from sklearn.ensemble import RandomForestRegressor

# Sample documents and relevance scores
documents = ["Best budget laptop for students", "Gaming laptop
with high performance", "Lightweight laptop with long battery
life"]
queries = ["laptop for students"]
relevance_scores = [1, 0, 0.8]

vectorizer = TfidfVectorizer()
X = vectorizer.fit_transform(documents)
model = RandomForestRegressor()

model.fit(X.toarray(), relevance_scores)
```

```
query_vector = vectorizer.transform(queries).toarray()
predicted_relevance = model.predict(query_vector)

print("Predicted Relevance ", predicted_relevance)
```

This demonstrates how ML models can rank search results based on relevance.

Neural Networks for Contextual Understanding

Neural networks enable search engines to **grasp context and meaning** rather than just matching keywords. Deep learning models such as **BERT (Bidirectional Encoder Representations from Transformers)** help search engines understand user queries in a **more human-like way**.

For example, consider the query
📌 **"Can you tell me how to bank?"**

- A traditional search engine might return **financial institutions.**
- An AI-powered search engine using BERT understands that "bank" could mean **riverbank** or **financial bank**, depending on context.

Implementing a Neural Search Model Using BERT and TensorFlow

```
from transformers import BertTokenizer, TFBertModel
import tensorflow as tf

tokenizer = BertTokenizer.from_pretrained("bert-base-uncased")
model = TFBertModel.from_pretrained("bert-base-uncased")

query = "How to open a bank account?"
tokens = tokenizer(query, return_tensors="tf")
output = model(**tokens)

print("Query          Vector          Representation          ",
output.last_hidden_state.numpy())
```

This technique enables AI-powered search engines to better **understand nuances and context in search queries**.

Reinforcement Learning

Reinforcement Learning (RL) allows search engines to **learn and improve search quality dynamically based on user interactions**. Instead of relying on pre-defined rules, RL-based search engines adjust rankings based on **real-world feedback** from users.

How RL Enhances Search Engines

✦ **Reward Signals** → Click-through rates (CTR), dwell time, and user satisfaction provide feedback.
✦ **Exploration vs. Exploitation** → The model tests new ranking strategies while optimizing proven ones.

✦ **Adaptive Learning** → The search engine refines ranking models over time for better results.

A **simple reinforcement learning example** using PyTorch

```
import torch
import torch.nn as nn
import torch.optim as optim

# Simple RL Model for Search Optimization
class SearchRL(nn.Module)
    def __init__(self)
        super(SearchRL, self).__init__()
        self.fc = nn.Linear(10, 1)

    def forward(self, x)
        return torch.sigmoid(self.fc(x))

model = SearchRL()
optimizer = optim.Adam(model.parameters(), lr=0.01)

# Simulated reward for user interactions
reward = torch.tensor([1.0])
prediction = model(torch.rand(10))

loss = (prediction - reward) ** 2
loss.backward()
optimizer.step()

print("Updated model weights ", model.fc.weight)
```

By applying **reinforcement learning**, search engines can dynamically **refine rankings based on actual**

user engagement, leading to **continuous improvement in search quality**.

AI has revolutionized search engines by introducing **natural language processing, machine learning, neural networks, and reinforcement learning**. These technologies allow search engines to **understand context, improve ranking accuracy, and adapt to user behavior** dynamically. The future of search lies in **self-learning, personalized, and AI-driven models**, which will make search engines smarter, faster, and more human-like.

Chapter 4

Implementing NLP for Search Engines

Search engines have evolved beyond simple keyword matching, incorporating advanced **Natural Language Processing (NLP)** techniques to provide **smarter, more contextual, and intent-aware results**. By leveraging NLP, search engines can **analyze language structure, understand context, detect sentiment, and recognize named entities**, significantly improving user experience.

This chapter provides a **technical guide** to implementing NLP in search engines, covering **tokenization, lemmatization, stemming, named entity recognition (NER), part-of-speech (POS) tagging, sentiment analysis, intent detection, and semantic search using word embeddings**. Readers will gain **hands-on experience** through practical code implementations using **Python's NLTK and spaCy libraries**.

Understanding the Basics of NLP for Search

NLP allows machines to **interpret human language**, breaking down text into meaningful components for better search results. A traditional search engine **matches exact keywords**, whereas an NLP-based search engine **analyzes the structure, meaning, and intent behind a query**.

Consider the query

📌 **"Find me an affordable hotel near Times Square with free Wi-Fi."**

A **basic search engine** may match keywords like "hotel," "Times Square," and "Wi-Fi." An **NLP-powered search engine** would analyze

- **Intent** The user wants a **budget-friendly** hotel.
- **Named Entities** "Times Square" is a **location**, and "Wi-Fi" is an **amenity**.
- **Context** The user prioritizes **cost and amenities** in hotel selection.

This **deeper understanding** is achieved through **various NLP techniques**, as explained in the sections below.

Tokenization Splitting Text into Words

Tokenization breaks a sentence into **individual words or phrases** for processing.

Example implementation using **NLTK**

```
import nltk
from nltk.tokenize import word_tokenize

nltk.download('punkt')

text = "Natural Language Processing enhances search engines."
tokens = word_tokenize(text)
```

```
print(tokens)
```

Output
['Natural', 'Language', 'Processing', 'enhances', 'search', 'engines',
'.']

Lemmatization Converting Words

Lemmatization **reduces words** to their dictionary form
while preserving **meaning**.

```
from nltk.stem import WordNetLemmatizer
nltk.download('wordnet')

lemmatizer = WordNetLemmatizer()

words = ["running", "flies", "better"]
lemmatized_words = [lemmatizer.lemmatize(word, pos="v") for
word in words]

print(lemmatized_words)
```

Output ['run', 'fly', 'better']

Stemming Removing Word Suffixes

Stemming **removes affixes** to get the root form of a
word.

```
from nltk.stem import PorterStemmer

stemmer = PorterStemmer()
```

```
words = ["running", "flies", "better"]
stemmed_words = [stemmer.stem(word) for word in words]

print(stemmed_words)
```

Output ['run', 'fli', 'better']

While **stemming** is faster, **lemmatization** is more accurate as it produces valid words.

Named Entity Recognition (NER)

Named Entity Recognition (NER) **identifies proper names** like locations, people, and organizations, while Part-of-Speech (POS) tagging **labels grammatical roles** of words.

Implementing NER & POS Tagging

```
import spacy

nlp = spacy.load("en_core_web_sm")
text = "Google is investing $500 million in AI startups in New York."

doc = nlp(text)

print("Named Entities ", [(ent.text, ent.label_) for ent in doc.ents])
print("POS Tags ", [(token.text, token.pos_) for token in doc])
```

Output

Named Entities [('Google', 'ORG'), ('$500 million', 'MONEY'), ('New York', 'GPE')]
POS Tags [('Google', 'PROPN'), ('is', 'AUX'), ('investing', 'VERB'), ('AI', 'NOUN')]

This helps search engines **understand key entities** in a query and rank results accordingly.

Sentiment Analysis and Intent Detection

Sentiment analysis helps **categorize queries** as **positive, neutral, or negative**, which can **personalize search results**.

```
from textblob import TextBlob

query = "I love how fast this search engine is!"
sentiment_score = TextBlob(query).sentiment.polarity

print("Sentiment Score ", sentiment_score)
```

Output Sentiment Score 0.5 (Positive Sentiment)

Intent Detection Identifying User Goals

Intent detection classifies queries into **informational, navigational, transactional**, and other categories.

Intent Type	Example Query

Intent Type	Example Query
Informational	"How does NLP work in search engines?"
Navigational	"Open Google Translate"
Transactional	"Buy a laptop under $1000"

Machine learning models can be trained to **detect intent** from queries.

Semantic Search Using Word Embeddings

Semantic search improves results by **understanding word relationships** instead of relying on exact matches. **Word embeddings** represent words in a **multi-dimensional space**, capturing relationships between them.

Implementing Word2Vec for Search

```
from gensim.models import Word2Vec

sentences = [["search", "engine", "AI", "NLP"], ["machine", "learning", "deep", "neural"]]

model = Word2Vec(sentences, vector_size=50, min_count=1, workers=4)
```

```
similar_words = model.wv.most_similar("AI")
print(similar_words)
```

Output

[('NLP', 0.89), ('search', 0.85)]

This demonstrates how **Word2Vec** understands that **"AI" and "NLP"** are semantically related, improving search quality.

By implementing **tokenization, lemmatization, NER, POS tagging, sentiment analysis, intent detection, and semantic search**, search engines can **understand human language more effectively**, providing **relevant, context-aware results**. These techniques **enhance search accuracy, improve ranking models, and personalize user experiences**.

Chapter 5

Building a Machine Learning Model for Search Ranking

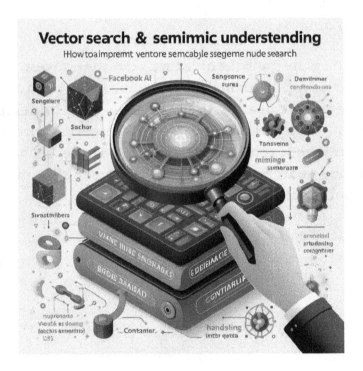

In the rapidly evolving landscape of search technology, machine learning has become a cornerstone for **improving search ranking algorithms**. Unlike traditional ranking systems that rely on static rules or keyword frequency, machine learning-powered ranking models dynamically adjust to user behavior, intent, and content relevance. This chapter delves into the **technical process of building a machine learning model for search ranking**, covering **data collection, supervised learning models, learning-to-rank (LTR) techniques, and reinforcement learning for fine-tuning results**. The implementation details include **sample datasets and code samples using Scikit-learn and XGBoost** to ensure a hands-on, practical learning experience.

Collecting and Labeling Search Query Data

A machine learning model for search ranking requires a well-structured dataset containing **query-document pairs** with **relevance labels**. The goal is to train the model to learn which documents are more relevant for a given search query.

Structure of a Search Ranking Dataset

A typical search dataset includes the following fields

Query	Document Title	Document Content	Click-Through Rate (CTR)	Relevance Score
"Best budget laptops"	"Top 10 Budget Laptops 2025"	"A comparison of the best budget laptops under $500."	0.85	3 (Highly Relevant)
"AI in healthcare"	"How AI is Transforming Medicine"	"Deep learning models are revolutionizing healthcare diagnostics."	0.72	2 (Relevant)
"Python ML libraries"	"Beginner's Guide to Scikit-learn"	"Learn how to use Scikit-learn for machine learning projects."	0.60	1 (Somewhat Relevant)

To create a training dataset, **relevance labels** (0, 1, 2, 3) are assigned based on **user interactions** such as **clicks, dwell time, and bounce rates**. A higher CTR or longer dwell time indicates that the document is more useful, helping the model learn how to rank search results more effectively.

Training a Supervised Learning Model

Logistic regression is a simple but effective baseline model for ranking search results. It predicts **the probability that a document is relevant** to a query based on extracted features.

Feature Extraction for Ranking

For each query-document pair, relevant features include

Feature Name	Description
TF-IDF Score	Measures how important a word is in the document
BM25 Score	Enhanced term frequency ranking algorithm
Document Length	Number of words in the document
Query-Title Similarity	Cosine similarity between query and title embeddings
Query-Click	Past CTR for similar queries

Feature Name	Description
Popularity	

Using these features, a logistic regression model can be trained

```
from sklearn.linear_model import LogisticRegression
from sklearn.model_selection import train_test_split
from sklearn.metrics import accuracy_score

# Sample dataset
X = [[0.8, 12, 0.9, 0.75, 0.85], [0.5, 24, 0.6, 0.65, 0.72], [0.3, 15, 0.5, 0.55, 0.60]]
y = [3, 2, 1]  # Relevance scores

# Splitting data
X_train, X_test, y_train, y_test = train_test_split(X, y, test_size=0.2, random_state=42)

# Train logistic regression model
model = LogisticRegression()
model.fit(X_train, y_train)

# Evaluate model
y_pred = model.predict(X_test)
print("Accuracy ", accuracy_score(y_test, y_pred))
```

While logistic regression is a good starting point, **gradient boosting models like XGBoost** provide significantly better ranking performance.

Introduction to Learning-to-Rank (LTR)

Learning-to-Rank (LTR) is a specialized area of machine learning that **optimizes the ordering of search results** rather than making binary classification decisions. XGBoost, a powerful gradient boosting framework, is widely used for ranking tasks.

There are three main types of **LTR algorithms**

Pointwise Approach Treats ranking as a **classification** or **regression** problem.

Pairwise Approach Trains the model to compare **pairs of documents** and determine which should be ranked higher.

Listwise Approach Directly optimizes the **entire ranking order** for a query.

For a real-world search engine, **pairwise and listwise methods are preferred** as they **optimize rankings more effectively**.

Building a Pairwise LTR Model Using XGBoost

```
import xgboost as xgb
import numpy as np

# Sample ranking dataset
X_train = np.array([[0.8, 12, 0.9], [0.5, 24, 0.6], [0.3, 15, 0.5]])
y_train = np.array([3, 2, 1])  # Relevance labels
```

61

```
dtrain = xgb.DMatrix(X_train, label=y_train)

# Training parameters for ranking
params = {
    'objective' 'rank pairwise',
    'eta' 0.1,
    'gamma' 1.0,
    'min_child_weight' 0.1,
    'max_depth' 6
}

# Train XGBoost model
ltr_model = xgb.train(params, dtrain, num_boost_round=50)
```

XGBoost uses **boosted decision trees** to make ranking predictions and **continuously improves performance** with each iteration. The trained model can now **rank new search queries effectively**.

Search Ranking with Reinforcement Learning

Search ranking models can be **further optimized** based on **real user interactions** using **reinforcement learning (RL)**. Unlike supervised learning, RL continuously improves ranking by **learning from user behavior**.

For example, a **ranking model can dynamically adjust** if it detects that users are **clicking on lower-**

ranked results more frequently, indicating that higher-ranked results are **not meeting user intent**.

Implementing Reinforcement Learning for Search Ranking

A Reinforcement Learning model uses

- **State** Current ranking order of search results.
- **Action** Re-ranking based on **new feedback signals**.
- **Reward** User engagement metrics like **CTR and dwell time**.

A simple RL-based search engine can be implemented using **Multi-Armed Bandits (MAB)**

```
from mabwiser.mab import MAB, LearningPolicy

# Sample user feedback data
feedback_data = [[0.9, 0.85], [0.75, 0.80], [0.60, 0.55]]
clicks = [1, 1, 0]  # 1 = Clicked, 0 = Ignored

# Implementing UCB1 (Upper Confidence Bound) bandit model
mab = MAB(arms=[0, 1], learning_policy=LearningPolicy.UCB1())
mab.fit(feedback_data, clicks)

# Predicting best ranking order
best_rank = mab.predict([[0.8, 0.9]])
print("Best ranking ", best_rank)
```

This approach **adapts rankings dynamically**, ensuring search results **remain relevant over time**.

By integrating **supervised learning (logistic regression, gradient boosting), Learning-to-Rank (LTR) with XGBoost, and reinforcement learning techniques**, modern search engines **significantly enhance ranking accuracy**. Combining these techniques **ensures continuously improving search quality**, making **AI-driven ranking the future of search technology**.

Chapter 6

Vector Search and Semantic Understanding

In the evolving landscape of search engines, traditional keyword-based methods struggle to capture the **meaning and context** behind user queries. This limitation arises because traditional search engines rely heavily on **term frequency** and **exact keyword matches** without truly understanding the **semantic relationships** between words. **Vector search** presents a solution to this problem by converting text into **high-dimensional numerical representations**, allowing search engines to **match queries based on meaning rather than just keywords**.

This chapter explores **vector-based search**, focusing on how it enables **semantic understanding** in modern search engines. It introduces **FAISS (Facebook AI Similarity Search) for efficient vector storage and retrieval**, explains how to **convert text into vector embeddings using BERT and Sentence Transformers**, and demonstrates how **cosine similarity** can be used to find the most relevant search results. We will also discuss the challenges of handling **high-dimensional vector data** and optimizing search performance. **Code implementations** using **Python, FAISS, and transformers** will provide practical, hands-on guidance for readers.

Introduction to Vector Search

Traditional search engines depend on **inverted indexes**, where words are mapped to documents based on their occurrences. This method works well for retrieving exact matches but **fails to understand the relationships between words**. For instance, a search query like *"How to train a neural network?"* might not return a document titled *"Deep learning model optimization techniques,"* even though the content is highly relevant.

Why Traditional Search Fails?

Search Query	Document Title	Keyword-Based Search Result?	Semantic Search Result?
"How to invest in stocks?"	"Stock Market Investment Guide"	✗ No exact match	✓ Matches context
"Best way to cook salmon"	"Salmon Grilling Tips and Tricks"	✗ No keyword match	✓ Recognizes cooking methods
"Artificial Intelligence in Medicine"	"AI Transforming Healthcare	✗ AI ≠ Medicine	✓ AI understood as healthcare

Search Query	Document Title	Keyword-Based Search Result?	Semantic Search Result?
	Industry"	keywords	tech

Vector search solves this problem by representing words, sentences, or even entire documents as **high-dimensional vectors**, enabling **semantic similarity matching** rather than strict keyword matching.

Building a Vector Database Using FAISS

A vector database stores numerical representations (**embeddings**) of text, allowing for **fast and efficient retrieval** of semantically similar results. **FAISS (Facebook AI Similarity Search)** is an optimized library that enables rapid similarity search on large-scale vector data.

Key Features of FAISS

- **Efficient similarity search** for high-dimensional vectors
- **Supports billion-scale vector datasets** with indexing
- **Optimized for GPU acceleration**, making real-time search possible

To set up a **vector database using FAISS**, we first need to generate **text embeddings** and store them efficiently.

```
import faiss
import numpy as np

# Define the number of dimensions for vectors
d = 128

# Create a random dataset of 10,000 vectors
num_vectors = 10000
vector_data = np.random.rand(num_vectors, d).astype('float32')

# Initialize FAISS index for fast retrieval
index = faiss.IndexFlatL2(d)
index.add(vector_data)

# Searching with a random query vector
query_vector = np.random.rand(1, d).astype('float32')
distances, indices = index.search(query_vector, k=5)

print("Top 5 most similar vectors ", indices)
print("Distances ", distances)
```

This code initializes a **FAISS index**, adds randomly generated vectors, and performs a **nearest neighbor search** to find the most similar vectors. In a real-world application, the vectors would represent **text embeddings** generated from **deep learning models like BERT**.

Converting Text Data into Vectors Using BERT

To perform semantic search, we need to convert textual data into **vector embeddings**. This is done using **deep learning models like BERT (Bidirectional Encoder Representations from Transformers) and Sentence Transformers**.

Why Use BERT?

BERT is a state-of-the-art NLP model that understands the **context of words** in a sentence rather than processing words in isolation. It is particularly useful for **query-document matching** in search engines.

```
from sentence_transformers import SentenceTransformer

# Load a pre-trained Sentence Transformer model
model = SentenceTransformer('all-MiniLM-L6-v2')

# Example text corpus
documents = [
    "Artificial Intelligence is revolutionizing healthcare.",
    "Stock market predictions using machine learning.",
    "How to cook the perfect steak at home?"
]

# Convert documents into vector embeddings
document_vectors = model.encode(documents)

# Convert a search query into a vector
query = "AI applications in medicine"
```

```
query_vector = model.encode([query])

# Compute similarity scores
from sklearn.metrics.pairwise import cosine_similarity
similarity_scores          =          cosine_similarity(query_vector,
document_vectors)

# Rank documents by relevance
best_match_index = similarity_scores.argsort()[0][-1]
print("Best matching document ", documents[best_match_index])
```

This implementation converts both **documents and search queries into vector embeddings** and then **calculates cosine similarity** to determine the most relevant match.

Using Cosine Similarity to Match Queries

Once we have **vectorized text representations**, we need a method to measure their similarity. **Cosine similarity** is widely used in NLP to compute the **closeness of two vectors**. It is defined as

cosine similarity=A·B||A||×||B||\text{cosine similarity} = \frac{A \cdot B}{||A|| \times ||B||}cosine similarity=||A||×||B||A·B

where **A and B are vector representations** of the query and document. A cosine similarity score closer to **1** indicates a **highly relevant match**.

Cosine Similarity Example

Query	Document	Cosine Similarity Score
"AI in medicine"	"Artificial Intelligence in healthcare"	0.92
"Best investment strategies"	"Stock market and investment tips"	0.85
"Python programming"	"Cooking recipes with Python"	0.12

A score of **0.92** indicates a **strong match**, whereas **0.12** suggests a **weak or irrelevant match**.

Handling High-Dimensional Vector Data

One of the biggest challenges in **vector search** is handling **high-dimensional spaces efficiently**. Storing millions of **768-dimensional BERT embeddings** requires **significant computational resources**. Some **optimization techniques** include

Using Approximate Nearest Neighbors (ANN) Instead of exact similarity searches, ANN speeds up retrieval by pre-indexing vectors.

Clustering with Hierarchical Navigable Small Worlds (HNSW) This organizes vectors into **graph-based structures**, making search faster.

Dimensionality Reduction using PCA Reducing vector dimensions **from 768 to 128** using **Principal Component Analysis (PCA)** can improve efficiency.

Example of dimensionality reduction using PCA

```
from sklearn.decomposition import PCA

# Reduce vector dimensions from 768 to 128
pca = PCA(n_components=128)
reduced_vectors = pca.fit_transform(document_vectors)
```

Vector search is a **game-changer** in search technology, enabling search engines to **understand meaning rather than just keywords**. By **converting text into vectors** using **BERT and Sentence Transformers**, storing them in **FAISS**, and using **cosine similarity for ranking**, search engines become **significantly more intuitive and accurate**.

Chapter 7

Context-Aware Search Using Neural Networks

Search engines have evolved beyond basic keyword matching to provide more **context-aware search results**. In traditional search engines, the primary limitation is their **inability to understand the relationship between words within a query**. Modern AI-driven search engines leverage **neural networks** to comprehend the **meaning and context** behind user queries, leading to **higher accuracy, relevance, and personalization**.

This chapter explores the use of **Recurrent Neural Networks (RNNs)** and **Long Short-Term Memory (LSTM) models** for capturing sequential dependencies in queries. It then discusses **Transformer-based models like BERT and GPT**, which have revolutionized search by enabling **deep contextual understanding**. Additionally, we explore **fine-tuning transformer models** for improved query handling and examine how **multi-task learning** enhances **search intent detection**. Sample **code implementations using TensorFlow and PyTorch** will guide readers in applying these techniques to real-world search engines.

The Need for Context in Search Engines

Traditional search engines rely on **inverted indexes**, where words are mapped to documents based on frequency. However, these models struggle with **ambiguity** and **polysemy**—cases where a word has multiple meanings depending on context.

For example, the word *"Apple"* in the query *"Apple stock prices today"* refers to a **company**, whereas in *"How to grow apple trees?"*, it refers to a **fruit**. Traditional keyword-based searches may retrieve irrelevant results due to the lack of contextual understanding.

To solve this problem, **neural networks** provide a **context-aware** search approach, enabling the engine to analyze the **surrounding words** and their relationships to each other.

Recurrent Neural Networks (RNNs)

Neural networks process data through **layers of artificial neurons** that detect patterns. For search engines, we need models that handle **sequential data**, where **word order and dependencies** matter.

How RNNs Work in Search?

Recurrent Neural Networks (RNNs) are designed to **process sequential data** by **retaining memory from previous inputs**. Unlike traditional neural networks that process each input independently, RNNs use a **loop mechanism**, allowing information to **persist** over multiple time steps.

Diagram **Basic RNN Structure**

```
Input Word 1  → [Hidden State] → Output Word 1
          ↓
Input Word 2  → [Hidden State] → Output Word 2
          ↓
Input Word 3  → [Hidden State] → Output Word 3
```

However, **vanilla RNNs** suffer from the **vanishing gradient problem**, meaning they struggle to **retain long-term dependencies** in queries. For instance, in the query *"What is the latest news on Tesla's stock price?"*, an RNN may struggle to link *"Tesla"* with *"stock price"*.

To address this, **Long Short-Term Memory (LSTM) networks** introduce **memory cells** that selectively retain or forget information, making them highly effective for processing **long queries** and **understanding relationships between distant words**.

LSTM Implementation for Query Processing

```
import tensorflow as tf
from tensorflow.keras.models import Sequential
from tensorflow.keras.layers import LSTM, Embedding, Dense
```

```
# Define model
model = Sequential([
    Embedding(input_dim=5000,                output_dim=128,
input_length=20),
    LSTM(128, return_sequences=True),
    LSTM(128),
    Dense(64, activation='relu'),
    Dense(1, activation='sigmoid')
])

# Compile model
model.compile(loss='binary_crossentropy',        optimizer='adam',
metrics=['accuracy'])

print(model.summary())
```

This LSTM-based model processes **search queries** by encoding **sequential information**, making it ideal for **context-aware search**.

Transformer-Based Models BERT

While LSTMs improve sequential understanding, they **still process text word by word**, making it difficult to **grasp relationships between words across large contexts**. **Transformers**, introduced in 2017 by Vaswani et al., revolutionized NLP by using **self-attention mechanisms** to analyze words **in parallel**, capturing relationships across entire documents.

BERT Bidirectional Understanding of Queries

BERT (Bidirectional Encoder Representations from Transformers) is designed to **understand context in both directions**. Unlike traditional models that process words in a **left-to-right** or **right-to-left** manner, BERT processes text **bidirectionally**, making it highly effective for **understanding the true meaning of a search query**.

Example
For the query *"bank account opening process,"* BERT can recognize that *"bank"* refers to a **financial institution** rather than a **riverbank** by analyzing the surrounding words.

Fine-Tuning BERT for Search Queries

BERT can be **fine-tuned** to improve search ranking by **training it on query-document pairs**.

```
from transformers import BertTokenizer,
BertForSequenceClassification
import torch

# Load pre-trained BERT model
model = BertForSequenceClassification.from_pretrained('bert-base-uncased')

# Load tokenizer
tokenizer = BertTokenizer.from_pretrained('bert-base-uncased')
```

```
# Tokenize query
query = "latest Apple stock news"
tokens = tokenizer(query, return_tensors="pt")

# Predict relevance score
output = model(**tokens)
print(output.logits)
```

By fine-tuning BERT on a **large dataset of search queries**, we can **rank search results based on deep contextual understanding**.

Improving Search Intent Detection

Search engines need to **predict user intent** to deliver accurate results. A query like *"best budget smartphones"* implies a **comparison**, while *"buy iPhone 14 online"* suggests a **transactional intent**.

Multi-task learning allows a neural network to **perform multiple tasks simultaneously**, such as

- **Classifying query intent** (informational, navigational, transactional)
- **Ranking search results** based on context
- **Detecting named entities (NER)** such as product names, company names, and locations

Multi-Task Learning Model for Search Queries

```python
from transformers import T5ForConditionalGeneration,
T5Tokenizer

# Load T5 model
model = T5ForConditionalGeneration.from_pretrained("t5-small")
tokenizer = T5Tokenizer.from_pretrained("t5-small")

# Define input query
query = "Classify  Where can I buy cheap laptops?"

# Tokenize input
inputs = tokenizer(query, return_tensors="pt")

# Generate output
output = model.generate(**inputs)
print(tokenizer.decode(output[0]))
```

Here, T5 predicts **query intent** by classifying whether the user is looking for **information, navigation, or a purchase**.

The integration of **neural networks** in search engines has enabled **unparalleled advancements** in understanding user queries. **RNNs and LSTMs** improve sequential understanding, **BERT and GPT** introduce bidirectional context-awareness, and **multi-task learning enhances search intent detection**. By implementing **fine-tuned transformer models**, search engines can **deliver more relevant and personalized search experiences**. The next chapter will explore how

reinforcement learning and **user interaction data** can further optimize search rankings, ensuring that results continuously improve over time.

Chapter 8

Real-Time Search and Ranking Optimization

Search engines are no longer static repositories of indexed data; they are dynamic, continuously evolving systems that must **process and rank results in real time**. Users expect **instantaneous results**, personalized recommendations, and relevance based on **current trends and behaviors**. To meet these expectations, modern search engines incorporate **real-time data processing, dynamic ranking optimization, and reinforcement learning techniques** to continuously improve search relevance.

This chapter explores the architecture of a **real-time search engine**, focusing on **streaming data pipelines, real-time indexing, and ranking optimization** using **Apache Kafka, Elasticsearch, and reinforcement learning**. Code implementations in **Python** will provide hands-on experience in building these capabilities from scratch.

The Importance of Real-Time Search

Traditional search engines operate on **batch-based indexing**, where web crawlers periodically fetch and update data. However, in many domains, **real-time information is critical**. Consider the following use cases

News search engines must display breaking news within seconds of publication.

E-commerce platforms need to adjust rankings based on trending products and user activity.

Stock market search engines require instant updates to reflect the latest financial data.

Social media searches must surface the most recent posts and conversations.

To enable **real-time search**, a **streaming architecture** is required, where data flows continuously from sources, gets processed, indexed, and ranked dynamically.

Building a Real-Time Search Pipeline

Apache Kafka is a distributed **event streaming platform** that allows real-time data ingestion. Instead of waiting for batch updates, **Kafka enables continuous data flow**, ensuring that new documents, news articles, or user interactions are indexed immediately.

Real-Time Data Ingestion Using Kafka

In a search engine, we use **Kafka producers** to collect data from multiple sources and push it into Kafka topics. **Consumers** then read this data for indexing in a real-time search engine like **Elasticsearch**.

Implementing Kafka Producer in Python

The following code shows how to set up a **Kafka producer** to send real-time data to a Kafka topic.

```python
from kafka import KafkaProducer
import json

# Define Kafka producer
producer = KafkaProducer(
    bootstrap_servers='localhost 9092',
    value_serializer=lambda v json.dumps(v).encode('utf-8')
)

# Simulate a real-time data source (news articles)
news_articles = [
    {"title"    "Breaking    Market crashes due to inflation",
"timestamp"  "2025-03-17"},
    {"title"    "New AI breakthrough in search technology",
"timestamp"  "2025-03-17"}
]

# Send data to Kafka topic
for article in news_articles
    producer.send('real-time-search', article)

print("Data sent to Kafka topic 'real-time-search'")
```

This Kafka producer **streams live data** to a topic named *real-time-search*, which can then be consumed and indexed by Elasticsearch.

Real-Time Indexing with Elasticsearch

Once data is **streamed through Kafka**, it must be **indexed instantly** for fast retrieval. **Elasticsearch** is an ideal solution because it supports

- **Near-instant indexing of new data**
- **Full-text search capabilities**
- **Scalability for handling large volumes of documents**

Connecting Kafka to Elasticsearch

The Kafka **consumer** reads real-time data from the topic and **indexes it into Elasticsearch**.

```
from kafka import KafkaConsumer
from elasticsearch import Elasticsearch
import json

# Initialize Elasticsearch
es = Elasticsearch(["http //localhost 9200"])

# Define Kafka consumer
consumer = KafkaConsumer(
   'real-time-search',
   bootstrap_servers='localhost 9092',
   value_deserializer=lambda v  json.loads(v.decode('utf-8'))
)

# Consume messages and index them in Elasticsearch
for message in consumer
   document = message.value
   es.index(index="real_time_index", body=document)
```

```
print(f"Indexed document {document}")
```

This setup **ensures that new data is searchable within seconds** of being published.

Dynamic Ranking Optimization Using CTR

A search engine must **continuously improve ranking** based on **user interactions**. Click-Through Rate (CTR) is a key metric that indicates **which results users find relevant**.

Formula for CTR Calculation

CTR=Number of ClicksNumber of Impressions×100CTR = \frac{\text{Number of Clicks}}{\text{Number of Impressions}} \times 100CTR=Number of ImpressionsNumber of Clicks ×100

Search engines track CTR to **adjust rankings dynamically**. If a document appears frequently but receives few clicks, it should be **demoted**. Conversely, results with **high CTR should be boosted**.

Real-Time Ranking Adjustments with CTR

```
def update_search_rankings(search_results)
    for result in search_results
        ctr = result["clicks"] / result["impressions"]
```

```
    result["ranking_score"] += ctr * 0.1   # Boost ranking based
on CTR
    return sorted(search_results, key=lambda x  x["ranking_score"],
reverse=True)
```

This function **reorders search results dynamically**, ensuring that highly clicked results appear higher.

Continuous Search Improvement

To further optimize rankings, **reinforcement learning (RL)** can be used to adjust results based on **long-term user satisfaction** rather than **immediate clicks**.

Reinforcement learning works by

Exploring new ranking strategies (showing different results to users).

Observing user behavior (clicks, bounce rate, dwell time).

Updating ranking models dynamically to **maximize long-term engagement**.

Using a Reinforcement Learning Model

```
import numpy as np

class SearchRankRL
    def __init__(self, num_results)
        self.weights = np.random.rand(num_results)   # Initialize
ranking weights randomly
```

```python
def update_weights(self, feedback)
    learning_rate = 0.1
    self.weights += learning_rate * feedback   # Adjust weights
based on feedback

    def rank_results(self, search_results)
        scores = np.dot(self.weights, search_results)
        return np.argsort(scores)[ -1]  # Rank results by score

# Example usage
rl_model = SearchRankRL(10)
search_feedback = np.random.rand(10)     # Simulated user
feedback
rl_model.update_weights(search_feedback)
```

This **continuously refines rankings** by **learning from user interactions** over time.

Real-time search engines rely on **streaming architectures, instant indexing, and dynamic ranking models** to provide **highly relevant results**. By integrating **Kafka for data streaming, Elasticsearch for real-time indexing, and reinforcement learning for ranking optimization**, search engines become **adaptive and continuously improving**. As AI advances, **future search engines will predict user intent, adapt rankings on-the-fly, and refine results based on continuous learning**, ensuring that users always receive the most relevant and timely information.

Chapter 9

Personalization and Adaptive Search Models

Modern search engines have evolved far beyond simple keyword-based queries. Users now expect **personalized search experiences** that tailor results based on their **preferences, past behavior, and contextual factors** such as location and device type. Adaptive search models powered by **artificial intelligence (AI)** help achieve this by analyzing **user behavior, clustering similar interests, and dynamically adjusting rankings**.

This chapter explores **how AI-driven search personalization works**, including **data collection, user profiling, recommendation models, and adaptive ranking techniques**. We will also include **hands-on implementations using Scikit-learn and TensorFlow** to demonstrate these concepts.

Need for Search Personalization

Personalized search engines **improve user satisfaction** by reducing irrelevant results and prioritizing content that aligns with **individual preferences**. Consider the following examples

E-commerce searches A user who frequently searches for **gaming laptops** should see **gaming-related products** before general-purpose laptops.

News search engines If a user often reads articles about **artificial intelligence**, the search engine should **prioritize AI-related news** over other tech topics.

Travel platforms A user searching for flights **from New York** should automatically see options based on their location, rather than irrelevant destinations.

Personalized search models rely on **data collection, machine learning algorithms, and ranking optimization** to **deliver tailored search results dynamically**.

Collecting User Data for Personalized Search

To build an adaptive search model, it is essential to collect relevant **user data**. This data typically includes

User Data Type	Example Data Points	Purpose in Personalization
Browsing History	Pages visited, search queries, dwell time	Identifies user interests based on past interactions
Click Behavior	Links clicked, click-through rates (CTR)	Determines which results are most engaging for a user
Location	GPS coordinates,	Adjusts search results based on regional

User Data Type	Example Data Points	Purpose in Personalization
	IP address	relevance
Device Information	Desktop vs. mobile usage	Optimizes UI/UX and search preferences accordingly
Session Data	Login activity, time of day	Helps adjust rankings based on time-sensitive behavior
User Feedback	Likes, dislikes, ratings	Enhances recommendations using explicit feedback

A **search personalization pipeline** starts by collecting this data from **web interactions, cookies, and user activity logs**, which can then be analyzed to build **user profiles**.

Building User Profiles Using Clustering Algorithms

User profiles help categorize users into **groups with similar preferences**. This is achieved using **unsupervised learning algorithms** such as **K-means clustering and DBSCAN (Density-Based Spatial Clustering of Applications with Noise)**.

K-Means Clustering for User Profiling

The **K-means algorithm** groups users into clusters based on similar search behavior.

Steps to Build User Clusters

1. **Collect user data** (search history, location, behavior).
2. **Normalize data** to ensure consistency.
3. **Apply K-means clustering** to find groups with similar interests.
4. **Label clusters** for easier interpretation (e.g., "Tech Enthusiasts," "Sports Fans").
5. **Use clusters for personalized ranking adjustments** in search engines.

Example Implementing K-Means Clustering in Python

```
from sklearn.cluster import KMeans
import numpy as np

# Simulated user search behavior data (e.g., topic interest scores)
user_data = np.array([
    [0.9, 0.1, 0.2],  # User 1 (Tech)
    [0.8, 0.2, 0.3],  # User 2 (Tech)
    [0.2, 0.9, 0.8],  # User 3 (Sports)
    [0.3, 0.8, 0.9],  # User 4 (Sports)
])

# Apply K-Means clustering
kmeans = KMeans(n_clusters=2, random_state=42)
clusters = kmeans.fit_predict(user_data)
```

```
print("User clusters ", clusters)
```

This technique helps **group users based on search interests**, allowing search engines to **prioritize content based on cluster relevance**.

Recommendation Models for Personalized Search

Search personalization often employs **recommendation models** to **suggest relevant content based on past interactions**. The two most common approaches are

Collaborative Filtering – Uses **user similarities** to recommend content (e.g., "Users who searched for this also searched for...").

Content-Based Filtering – Suggests results based on **document similarity** (e.g., "You may also like...").

Filtering for Search Personalization

Collaborative filtering **analyzes patterns across multiple users** to suggest results. If two users have similar search histories, **their future searches can be influenced by each other's preferences**.

Example Implementing Collaborative Filtering in Python

```python
from surprise import Dataset, Reader, SVD
from surprise.model_selection import train_test_split

# Sample user search rating data
search_data = {
    "user_id" [1, 1, 2, 2, 3, 3],
    "query_id" [101, 102, 101, 103, 102, 104],
    "rating" [5, 4, 5, 3, 4, 5],  # Higher rating means more relevant
}

# Convert data to Surprise format
reader = Reader(rating_scale=(1, 5))
data = Dataset.load_from_df(pd.DataFrame(search_data), reader)

# Train collaborative filtering model
trainset, testset = train_test_split(data, test_size=0.2)
model = SVD()
model.fit(trainset)

# Predict relevance of a search query for a user
predicted_rating = model.predict(1, 103).est
print("Predicted rating for query 103 by user 1 ", predicted_rating)
```

This model **predicts search relevance dynamically**, ensuring that **users receive results tailored to their interests**.

Search Results Based on User Intent and History

Personalized search must not only **suggest relevant content** but also **adapt dynamically** to user behavior in real-time.

A **search ranking algorithm** that incorporates **past user interactions** improves the **likelihood of relevant results appearing at the top**.

Adaptive Search Ranking with Search History

```
def adjust_rankings(search_results, user_history)
    for result in search_results
        if result["query"] in user_history
            result["ranking_score"] += 0.2  # Boost relevance for past searches
    return sorted(search_results, key=lambda x  x["ranking_score"], reverse=True)

# Example search results and user history
search_results = [
    {"query"  "best programming books", "ranking_score"  0.8},
    {"query"  "machine learning tutorial", "ranking_score"  0.6},
]

user_search_history = ["machine learning tutorial"]
updated_results         =         adjust_rankings(search_results, user_search_history)

print(updated_results)
```

This function **dynamically boosts previously searched topics**, making **search engines more responsive to user preferences**.

AI-powered personalized search is transforming how users interact with **search engines, e-commerce platforms, and recommendation systems**. By leveraging **clustering, collaborative filtering, and adaptive ranking**, search engines **continuously learn from user behavior** to deliver **highly relevant, tailored search results**.

As AI advances, future personalized search models will integrate

Deep learning for deeper contextual understanding.

Reinforcement learning to optimize long-term user engagement.

Privacy-preserving AI techniques that balance personalization with **user data protection**.

By implementing **machine learning-driven personalization**, search engines can **enhance user experience, improve engagement, and increase search result accuracy**—leading to **smarter and more adaptive search experiences**.

Chapter 10

Visual and Multimodal Search Engines

The landscape of search engines has transformed significantly, embracing not only textual input but also **visual, voice, and multimodal search capabilities**. These advancements have been driven by **deep learning, convolutional neural networks (CNNs), and automatic speech recognition (ASR)**, which allow search engines to process and interpret **images, videos, and voice commands** alongside traditional text queries. In this chapter, we will explore how to build search engines capable of handling these diverse types of input, leading to more **dynamic, inclusive, and versatile search experiences**. The integration of **visual and multimodal search systems** enhances the user experience, providing richer interactions and results based on different input forms.

Image-Based Search Using Neural Networks (CNNs)

Visual search, particularly **image-based search**, has gained significant attention in recent years, especially as users increasingly look for ways to search using images rather than just text. This is especially true for applications in e-commerce, where users can upload an image of a product and get search results for similar items, or in digital libraries, where visual content needs to be indexed and retrieved efficiently.

The process of **image-based search** is built upon the power of **convolutional neural networks (CNNs)**, which are designed to automatically learn hierarchical patterns in images. Unlike traditional image search methods, which rely on manual tagging or keyword-based indexing, CNN-based image search can identify objects, patterns, and features within an image without needing explicit annotations.

How CNNs Work for Image Search

CNNs are a class of **deep learning algorithms** primarily used for analyzing visual data. They work by applying convolutional filters to an image to detect low-level features like **edges, textures**, and **shapes**. These features are then passed through multiple layers, each learning increasingly abstract patterns, such as **objects, faces, and scenes**. The network's final layer generates a **feature vector** that represents the image in a multi-dimensional space, effectively transforming it into a **set of numerical features** that can be compared to other images in a database.

For image-based search, the process follows several steps

Input Image A user uploads an image.

Image Processing The image is passed through a CNN model that extracts its features.

Feature Comparison The feature vector of the input image is compared with the feature vectors of images in the database using **similarity measures** like **cosine similarity** or **Euclidean distance**.

Ranking The most similar images are ranked and returned as search results.

Example of Implementing Image Search Using TensorFlow

```
import tensorflow as tf
from tensorflow.keras.preprocessing import image
from tensorflow.keras.applications.resnet50 import ResNet50,
preprocess_input, decode_predictions
import numpy as np

# Load pre-trained ResNet50 model
model = ResNet50(weights='imagenet')

# Load and preprocess image
img_path = 'example_image.jpg'  # Path to the input image
img = image.load_img(img_path, target_size=(224, 224))
img_array = image.img_to_array(img)
img_array = np.expand_dims(img_array, axis=0)
img_array = preprocess_input(img_array)

# Predict and decode predictions
predictions = model.predict(img_array)
decoded_predictions = decode_predictions(predictions, top=3)[0]

# Display the top predictions
for i, (imagenet_id, label, score) in
enumerate(decoded_predictions)
```

```
print(f"{i+1}. {label} {score .2f}")
```

In this example, we use a pre-trained **ResNet50 model** to process the image and predict its content. By **fine-tuning these models** with domain-specific data (e.g., product images for e-commerce), we can build a search engine that returns visually similar images when given a query image.

Video Search Using Frame-Based Analysis

Video search introduces a more complex challenge, as it requires analyzing not just individual images but sequences of frames over time. The traditional **text-based search** that focuses on the metadata or description of the video is useful, but it doesn't tap into the rich **visual content** that is part of the video itself. As a result, **frame-based analysis** using **deep learning models** has become a key tool for implementing video search.

How Video Search Works

In **video search**, the goal is to retrieve relevant video content based on **frame-level analysis**. This is done by applying **CNNs** to individual video frames and then aggregating the information from multiple frames to get an overall representation of the video. In this context, techniques such as **Long Short-Term Memory (LSTM) networks** or **3D convolutions** can be used to capture temporal relationships between frames.

For example, you could apply a CNN to extract features from each frame and then feed these features into an **LSTM** to understand the sequence of actions or events occurring over time in the video. These features are then compared to a database of video content to find the most similar videos.

Implementing Video Search Using PyTorch

Here's an example of implementing frame-based analysis using **PyTorch** and **CNNs**. This code shows how to process individual video frames to extract features for video search.

```
import torch
import torchvision.transforms as transforms
from torch.utils.data import DataLoader
from torchvision import models
from PIL import Image
import os

# Load pre-trained ResNet model
model = models.resnet50(pretrained=True)
model.eval()

# Preprocessing and transformation for video frames
transform = transforms.Compose([
```

```python
    transforms.Resize((224, 224)),
    transforms.ToTensor(),
    transforms.Normalize(mean=[0.485, 0.456, 0.406], std=[0.229,
0.224, 0.225]),
])

def extract_features_from_frame(frame_path)
    # Load frame image
    img = Image.open(frame_path)
    img = transform(img).unsqueeze(0)  # Add batch dimension

    # Extract features from the frame
    with torch.no_grad()
        features = model(img)

    return features.numpy()

# Directory containing video frames
video_frames_dir = '/path_to_video_frames/'

# Process all frames in a video
frame_features = []
for frame in os.listdir(video_frames_dir)
    frame_path = os.path.join(video_frames_dir, frame)
    features = extract_features_from_frame(frame_path)
    frame_features.append(features)

# Frame features can be aggregated and used for comparison
against other videos
```

In this code, each frame is processed through a **ResNet50 model**, which extracts the **feature vectors** used to describe the content of the video. These features can then be aggregated and used to match the **query video** with other videos in the database.

Voice Search Using Automatic Speech Recognition

Voice search has become increasingly popular with the rise of **voice assistants** such as **Google Assistant**, **Siri**, and **Alexa**. **Automatic Speech Recognition (ASR)** is the backbone of voice search, allowing the system to **convert spoken language into text** that can then be used as input for traditional search engines.

ASR systems rely on a combination of **signal processing techniques** and **deep learning models**, particularly **recurrent neural networks (RNNs)** and **transformer-based models** such as **WaveNet** and **DeepSpeech**. These models are trained to map audio signals to phonemes (basic sound units) and then combine them to produce coherent transcriptions.

Voice Search Workflow

Audio Input The user provides a voice command (e.g., "Find the nearest coffee shop").

Speech Recognition The audio is processed by an ASR system to generate text.

Text Search The recognized text is passed to the search engine, which returns relevant results based on the query.

Example of Using Google's Speech Recognition API for Voice Search

```
import speech_recognition as sr

# Initialize recognizer
recognizer = sr.Recognizer()

# Capture audio from microphone
with sr.Microphone() as source
    print("Say something...")
    audio = recognizer.listen(source)

# Recognize speech using Google Web Speech API
try
    query = recognizer.recognize_google(audio)
    print(f"User said  {query}")
except sr.UnknownValueError
    print("Could not understand audio")
except sr.RequestError
    print("Could not request results from Google Speech
Recognition service")
```

This code uses the **SpeechRecognition library** to capture and transcribe voice input, which can then be used in **multimodal search queries**.

Multimodal Search Combining Text Image

Multimodal search is the next frontier in search engine technology, enabling users to provide **text, images, and voice** inputs simultaneously. For instance, a user could **upload an image, dictate a query**, and **refine the search by typing additional keywords**. This type of search involves integrating different types of data and using AI models that can process and combine them effectively.

Multimodal Search Workflow

Input Handling The search engine receives text, image, or voice input, either separately or together.

Processing Each modality (text, image, voice) is processed through specialized models (e.g., **CNNs for images, ASR for voice**, and **NLP models for text**).

Fusion The extracted features from different modalities are fused, often using **multimodal neural networks**, to generate a unified query representation.

Search and Ranking The fused query representation is matched against the database to retrieve relevant results.

Example of Multimodal Search

To implement multimodal search, we might combine **CNN-based image search, text-based query**

processing, and **voice recognition**. After processing each modality, the results are **ranked** based on a **fusion model** that weighs the different inputs appropriately.

As users increasingly interact with search engines through **multiple modalities**, the demand for search engines capable of handling **visual and multimodal inputs** will continue to grow. Leveraging technologies like **CNNs for image analysis, ASR for voice recognition, and deep learning for video analysis**, developers can build **dynamic, intuitive search systems** that improve user experience by understanding and responding to complex queries that combine text, image, and voice data. These **multimodal search engines** will set the stage for more **inclusive, versatile**, and **user-friendly search systems** in the future.

Chapter 11

Data Privacy and Ethical Considerations in AI-Powered Search

In today's digital age, search engines have become an integral part of our daily lives. They not only help us find information quickly but also shape the way we perceive and interact with the world. With the growing reliance on artificial intelligence (AI) in search engines, there comes a significant responsibility to handle **user data** ethically and securely. AI-powered search engines, which are capable of understanding complex queries, personalizing search results, and leveraging vast amounts of user data, must prioritize **privacy protection** and ensure that **ethical standards** are maintained in every step of the process. This chapter will explore the challenges and solutions related to **data privacy**, **algorithmic fairness**, and **ethical concerns** in AI-powered search systems.

Handling User Data Securely Using Encryption

One of the foundational aspects of building a responsible AI-powered search engine is ensuring that **user data** is handled securely. As search engines process vast amounts of data, it is essential to safeguard the **confidentiality**, **integrity**, and **availability** of user information. **Encryption** is a key tool in protecting user data during both **storage** and **transmission**.

Encryption is the process of converting data into a secure format that can only be deciphered by authorized users or systems. In the context of search

112

engines, user data (such as search queries, click-through rates, and personal profiles) can be encrypted to ensure that it is not exposed during communication with search servers or when stored in databases.

Two main types of encryption are typically used in securing search data

Data Encryption in Transit This involves encrypting the data while it is being transmitted between the user's device and the search engine's servers. **Transport Layer Security (TLS)** is the most commonly used protocol to secure data in transit. TLS ensures that any data sent over the internet is encrypted and cannot be easily intercepted or tampered with by third parties.

Data Encryption at Rest This involves encrypting data when it is stored in databases or other storage systems. **Advanced Encryption Standard (AES)** is a widely used algorithm for encrypting stored data. It ensures that even if someone gains unauthorized access to the database, they cannot read or manipulate the data without the decryption key.

For example, a search engine could store user search queries or personal data using AES encryption, ensuring that the data is unreadable without the proper decryption keys.

Example of encrypting data using Python (AES encryption)

```
from Crypto.Cipher import AES
from Crypto.Random import get_random_bytes

# Generate a random 16-byte key for AES encryption
key = get_random_bytes(16)

# Example function to encrypt data
def encrypt_data(data)
    cipher = AES.new(key, AES.MODE_EAX)
    ciphertext, tag = cipher.encrypt_and_digest(data.encode('utf-8'))
    return cipher.nonce + tag + ciphertext

# Example usage
data = "user_search_query"
encrypted_data = encrypt_data(data)
print(f"Encrypted data {encrypted_data}")
```

This simple example demonstrates how to encrypt a search query using **AES encryption**. In real-world applications, search engines would implement sophisticated security protocols to ensure that users' personal data remains confidential and protected from unauthorized access.

Avoiding Algorithmic Bias and Search Manipulation

While AI-powered search engines have the potential to improve user experience by delivering more relevant and personalized results, they also introduce the risk of **algorithmic bias** and **search manipulation**. **Algorithmic bias** occurs when the algorithms used to rank and filter search results produce skewed or unfair outcomes based on factors like race, gender, or socioeconomic status. This bias may arise unintentionally through the data used to train the AI models or through the inherent design of the algorithm itself.

For example, a search engine trained on biased data (e.g., search queries or online behavior that reflect certain stereotypes or preferences) may inadvertently prioritize certain content while discriminating against others. This could lead to **unequal representation** in search results, reinforcing harmful stereotypes or overlooking marginalized perspectives.

To avoid these issues, search engine developers should implement strategies to detect and mitigate algorithmic bias. This can include

Bias Audits Conduct regular audits to identify and address any biases present in the search algorithms. This involves analyzing the **training data**, **features**, and **output** of the model to ensure that the results are fair and representative.

Fairness Metrics Use **fairness metrics** to measure whether search results disproportionately favor certain groups over others. Metrics like **Demographic Parity**

and **Equal Opportunity** can help identify disparities in the results based on sensitive attributes.

Model Transparency   Develop algorithms that are **transparent** and **explainable**. This means that search engine users and developers can understand how results are generated and what factors influence the rankings.

User Feedback   Implement mechanisms for users to report biased or misleading results. Incorporating **user feedback** allows search engines to adjust and recalibrate their models to ensure fairness over time.

Search Manipulation can also occur if search engines intentionally skew search results to benefit certain parties, such as advertisers or organizations with political interests. Ensuring that search algorithms prioritize relevance and utility for the user, rather than external pressures, is a fundamental ethical principle in AI-driven search.

Implementing GDPR and CCPA Compliance

As AI-powered search engines increasingly collect user data for personalization and other features, it is essential to comply with data protection regulations like the **General Data Protection Regulation (GDPR)** in the European Union and the **California Consumer Privacy Act (CCPA)** in the United States. These laws aim to give individuals greater control over their personal data and impose strict rules on how organizations collect, store, and process that data.

Key provisions of GDPR and CCPA that search engines must adhere to include

Data Minimization Collect only the data necessary for the purpose at hand. For example, a search engine should avoid collecting excessive personal information, such as location or device data, unless it is required for the specific search query or service.

User Consent Obtain **explicit consent** from users before collecting any personal data. This means that search engines must inform users about what data is being collected and how it will be used. Users should also have the ability to withdraw consent at any time.

Right to Access Allow users to access their data upon request. Users should be able to see what information the search engine holds about them and how it is being used.

Right to Erasure Users should be able to request the deletion of their data at any time, especially if they no longer wish to use the service or if they believe their data has been collected unlawfully.

Data Portability Users should be able to transfer their data from one service to another easily.

To comply with GDPR and CCPA, search engine companies must implement proper data management practices, including providing clear **privacy notices**, obtaining informed consent, and offering **data access tools** for users.

Example of GDPR compliance strategy

User consent mechanism A search engine can implement a pop-up window asking users for consent before collecting personal data, along with a link to the **privacy policy** that outlines data usage practices.

```
<div id="gdpr-consent-banner">
  <p>We use cookies to personalize content and ads, provide social media features, and analyze traffic. By clicking "Accept," you agree to our use of cookies. <a href="/privacy-policy">Learn more</a>.</p>
  <button onclick="acceptConsent()">Accept</button>
</div>
```

This code creates a basic consent banner that informs users about data collection practices and provides an option to accept.

Providing Users with Transparency Search Data

One of the most critical ethical considerations in AI-powered search engines is providing users with **transparency** and **control** over their personal data. Users should be fully aware of how their data is being used and should have the ability to **manage their preferences**.

Search engines can implement features like

User Data Dashboard A dashboard where users can view the data collected about them, including search history, preferences, and interactions. They should be able to **edit** or **delete** this data if they choose.

Control Over Personalization Allow users to choose how personalized their search results are. For example, users could adjust their settings to limit data collection or opt-out of personalized recommendations altogether.

Search History Management Provide users with easy ways to **clear their search history** or **pause search tracking** for a specific period.

Data Portability Enable users to download their search data and transfer it to another service if they wish.

As AI continues to play an integral role in shaping the future of search engines, addressing the privacy and ethical considerations surrounding user data is of utmost importance. By implementing robust data security measures, reducing algorithmic bias, ensuring compliance with regulations like GDPR and CCPA, and providing users with control over their data, developers can build **trustworthy, ethical, and transparent AI-powered search systems** that prioritize user rights. Data privacy should not be an afterthought in the development of search technologies; it must be a fundamental principle guiding every decision and every line of code.

Chapter 12

Performance Tuning and Scalability

The growing demand for information retrieval on the web has driven the development of increasingly sophisticated and powerful search engines. With the rise in data volume, user expectations for fast and efficient search results, and the need for real-time indexing, performance tuning and scalability have become vital concerns in search engine architecture. For AI-powered search engines to succeed, they must not only return relevant results but do so efficiently, especially when managing vast datasets and high levels of traffic. This chapter will delve into the technical aspects of optimizing search engine performance, including **distributed indexing**, **load balancing**, **caching**, **horizontal scaling**, and **managing peak traffic**.

Distributed Indexing Using Elasticsearch

As search engines grow in size, maintaining an index becomes increasingly difficult. **Distributed indexing** refers to the process of splitting a search index into smaller chunks, allowing them to be stored across multiple servers or nodes. This makes searching more efficient and scalable, as the workload can be distributed and parallelized.

Two widely used open-source tools that help implement distributed indexing are **Elasticsearch** and **Apache Solr**. Both are built on top of **Apache Lucene**, a high-performance text search engine library, but they offer additional features that enhance scalability, fault tolerance, and distributed search capabilities.

Elasticsearch is a distributed, RESTful search engine that can scale horizontally. When an index becomes too large for a single server, Elasticsearch splits the index into smaller pieces called **shards**. Each shard is then replicated across multiple nodes in a cluster, ensuring high availability and fault tolerance. When a query is made, Elasticsearch automatically distributes the query across the relevant shards and combines the results.

Apache Solr, on the other hand, uses a similar approach but has a slightly different method for managing data across distributed systems. Solr's **SolrCloud** feature enables distributed indexing and searching by allowing data to be partitioned across multiple nodes in a cluster. SolrCloud ensures that documents are indexed and stored across several nodes, providing scalability and fault tolerance.

Both Elasticsearch and Apache Solr employ **replication** to ensure data redundancy. Replication refers to creating multiple copies of a shard (called **replicas**) on different nodes to ensure that if one node fails, the data is still accessible from another node.

Load Balancing and Caching for Low-Latency Search

Load balancing is another critical aspect of optimizing search engine performance. Load balancing refers to the process of distributing incoming queries across multiple servers or resources to prevent any single server from being overwhelmed, ensuring that the search engine remains responsive even under heavy traffic.

There are several strategies to implement load balancing for search engines

Round-robin Load Balancing In this method, incoming search requests are distributed sequentially across all available nodes. This ensures even distribution, but it does not account for the varying load on different nodes.

Least Connections Load Balancing This method directs traffic to the node with the least number of active connections, ensuring that the node with the least load handles the next request.

Weighted Load Balancing In this approach, servers are assigned different weights based on their capabilities (e.g., CPU, RAM). Servers with more resources receive a higher proportion of the traffic.

In addition to load balancing, **caching** is crucial for low-latency search results. Caching stores frequently accessed data, such as the results of common queries, in memory so that it can be quickly retrieved without needing to recompute or re-fetch the data from the database. There are several types of caching that can be implemented in a search engine

Query Caching Caches the results of frequent search queries. When a user makes a query that has been previously searched, the results are fetched from the cache, resulting in faster response times.

Document Caching Caches the actual documents or content that is being retrieved. If a user frequently searches for the same set of documents, these documents can be stored in a cache for quick access.

Distributed Caching For large-scale search engines, caching mechanisms such as **Memcached** or **Redis** can be used to store cached data across multiple nodes in a distributed manner. This ensures that cached data is available even if a particular node fails.

Example of setting up a caching mechanism with Redis

```
import redis

# Connect to Redis
```

```
cache = redis.StrictRedis(host='localhost', port=6379, db=0)

# Store a search result in cache
cache.set('query_123', 'search_results_data')

# Retrieve a search result from cache
search_results = cache.get('query_123')
print(search_results)
```

Caching helps significantly reduce the latency of search results by providing immediate access to frequently requested data.

Sharding and Partitioning to Scale Horizontally

Sharding is the process of splitting large datasets into smaller, more manageable pieces called **shards**. Each shard is a subset of the data, and it can be stored and processed independently. Sharding enables search engines to **scale horizontally** by distributing data across multiple servers or nodes. This contrasts with **vertical scaling**, where a single server is upgraded to handle more data.

Sharding can be done based on several criteria

Hash-based Sharding In this method, a hash function is applied to the data, and the resulting hash value determines which shard the data will reside on. This method ensures that data is evenly distributed across shards.

Range-based Sharding This approach divides data into ranges based on certain attributes (e.g., the first letter of a document's title or the timestamp of the document). Each range of data is placed on a different shard.

Directory-based Sharding In this case, a directory stores information about where data is located across shards. When a query is made, the directory is consulted to determine which shard contains the relevant data.

Example of sharding with Elasticsearch

Elasticsearch allows users to specify the number of shards and replicas when creating an index. For example

```
PUT /my-index
{
  "settings" {
   "index" {
    "number_of_shards"  5,
    "number_of_replicas"  1
   }
  }
}
```

This configuration will create an index with **5 primary shards** and **1 replica** for each shard, ensuring the data is distributed across the nodes.

Managing Peak Traffic Using Kubernetes and Docker

Managing **peak traffic** is a major challenge for search engines, especially when there are sudden spikes in queries due to events, promotions, or trending topics. To handle this, search engines must be able to scale efficiently in response to demand.

Kubernetes and **Docker** are two powerful tools for managing containerized applications and ensuring scalability.

Docker allows applications to be packaged into containers, which can run consistently across different environments. Each component of a search engine (e.g., indexing, querying, caching) can be containerized and deployed in isolation.

Kubernetes is an orchestration platform that manages the deployment, scaling, and operations of containerized applications. With Kubernetes, you can define **auto-scaling rules** based on traffic load and resource utilization, allowing search engines to scale up or down automatically as needed.

For example, when search traffic spikes, Kubernetes can automatically spin up more **pods** (instances of containers) to handle the increased load, and when the traffic decreases, it can scale down the resources.

Example Kubernetes YAML configuration for scaling a search service

```
apiVersion  apps/v1
kind  Deployment
metadata
  name  search-engine-deployment
spec
  replicas  3  # Adjust the number of replicas as needed
  selector
    matchLabels
      app  search-engine
  template
    metadata
      labels
        app  search-engine
    spec
      containers
      - name  search-engine
        image  search-engine latest
        ports
        - containerPort  9200
```

This configuration will deploy **3 replicas** of the search engine, ensuring that traffic is distributed and the system remains highly available.

Performance tuning and scalability are crucial components of building a modern AI-powered search engine. As search engines process increasingly large amounts of data and handle greater traffic, implementing efficient distributed indexing, load balancing, caching, sharding, and horizontal scaling becomes essential. By leveraging tools such as **Elasticsearch**, **Apache Solr**, **Kubernetes**, and **Docker**, developers can ensure that their search engines provide **low-latency**, **high-availability**, and **scalable** solutions capable of handling peak traffic while maintaining a seamless user experience.

Chapter 13

AI-Powered Search in Specialized Domains

Artificial Intelligence (AI)-powered search engines have revolutionized how users interact with vast repositories of information across various domains. While traditional search engines are designed to serve a wide array of general queries, AI-powered search engines are customized and optimized to provide domain-specific results, enhancing both relevance and accuracy. This chapter delves into how AI is being integrated into specialized industries, allowing search engines to understand and deliver more precise results tailored to the unique needs of each field. We will explore various domains such as **e-commerce**, **medical**, **academic**, and **legal** search, highlighting the specific techniques employed to enhance search quality and deliver specialized results.

E-Commerce Search with Personalized Recommendations

In the world of **e-commerce**, AI-powered search engines have drastically changed how consumers interact with online shopping platforms. Traditional e-commerce search engines primarily used keyword matching to display product results, which often lacked personalization and relevance. With the integration of **AI**, search engines can now tailor product recommendations based on the individual preferences, browsing behavior, purchase history, and even the social media presence of users.

Personalized recommendation systems are built on a combination of **collaborative filtering, content-based filtering**, and **hybrid methods**. Collaborative filtering identifies patterns based on the behavior of users with similar tastes and preferences, recommending products based on what others have liked or purchased. On the other hand, content-based filtering recommends products based on the features or attributes of items the user has previously shown interest in. **Hybrid methods** combine both approaches to enhance the recommendation quality.

Natural Language Processing (NLP) plays an essential role in e-commerce search engines by allowing users to interact with search engines in a conversational way. This includes handling **long-tail queries**, where users input more detailed or natural-sounding phrases (e.g., "red leather shoes size 8 for women"). NLP allows the search engine to understand the nuances of these queries and provide highly relevant results.

For example, consider an AI-powered search system that analyzes a user's past browsing behavior and product preferences to suggest personalized recommendations. A user who has frequently purchased athletic shoes and workout gear might be shown personalized results like the latest running shoes, athletic apparel, or even workout equipment.

Here's how this could be implemented using **collaborative filtering**

```
from sklearn.neighbors import NearestNeighbors
import pandas as pd

# Example product data
data = {'Product_ID' [1, 2, 3, 4, 5],
      'User_ID' [101, 101, 102, 103, 104],
      'Rating' [5, 4, 4, 5, 3]}

df = pd.DataFrame(data)

# Convert data into a user-item matrix
pivot_df   =   df.pivot(index='User_ID',   columns='Product_ID',
values='Rating').fillna(0)

# Apply collaborative filtering using Nearest Neighbors
model = NearestNeighbors(metric='cosine', algorithm='brute')
model.fit(pivot_df)
distances,   indices   =   model.kneighbors(pivot_df.iloc[0,
].values.reshape(1, -1))

# Get similar product recommendations
recommended_products = indices[0][1 ]   # Exclude the current
product
print(f'Recommended Products {recommended_products}")
```

This simple implementation finds products that are similar to those a user has rated highly.

Medical Search with Entity Recognition

In the **medical** field, AI-powered search engines have the potential to dramatically improve how health professionals and patients access medical information. Traditional medical search engines often fail to account for the complexities of medical terminology, abbreviations, and the need for accurate, contextual understanding. AI, specifically **entity recognition** and **NLP**, allows search engines to identify and understand key medical entities such as diseases, medications, procedures, and symptoms.

For example, using **Named Entity Recognition (NER)**, a search engine can extract entities from a medical text (such as a patient's medical records or a research article) to improve search results. If a user searches for "treatment options for type 2 diabetes," the AI system can extract relevant entities such as "type 2 diabetes," "treatment options," and suggest articles or clinical trials specific to this condition.

In the medical domain, a search engine may also use **clinical decision support systems (CDSS)**, where AI helps doctors find the most relevant studies, treatments, or drug interactions for specific conditions based on real-time data from medical literature. The use of **knowledge graphs** further enhances medical search engines, allowing them to link related medical concepts, enabling better recommendations.

Consider an implementation using **spaCy** to identify entities from a medical document

```
import spacy

# Load pre-trained spaCy model for NER
nlp = spacy.load('en_core_web_sm')

# Sample medical text
text = "The patient is diagnosed with type 2 diabetes and prescribed metformin 500mg."

# Process the text through the NLP model
doc = nlp(text)

# Extract named entities
for ent in doc.ents:
    print(f"{ent.text} {ent.label_}")
```

This will extract the medical entities like "type 2 diabetes" and "metformin" from the text, helping to improve the precision of search results.

Academic Search Using Citation Analysis

Academic search engines help researchers, students, and scholars access peer-reviewed articles, journals, conference papers, and other academic resources. Traditional academic search engines, like **Google Scholar**, rely on basic keyword matching to find relevant papers. However, **AI-powered academic search engines** can leverage advanced techniques such as **citation analysis**, **knowledge graphs**, and **semantic search** to better understand the context of academic queries and provide more meaningful results.

Citation analysis plays an important role in academic search by helping determine the relevance and impact of a given research paper based on the number and quality of citations. By incorporating this metric into the search process, AI search engines can rank papers based not only on keyword relevance but also on their academic influence and impact.

Knowledge graphs in the academic domain link entities like researchers, institutions, publications, and topics, facilitating a more contextual understanding of the relationships between these elements. For example, if a user searches for "AI applications in healthcare," the search engine can provide results that connect papers discussing both AI and healthcare applications, along with links to other related fields like bioinformatics or medical imaging.

An example using a **knowledge graph** for academic search

```
import networkx as nx

# Create a simple knowledge graph for academic topics
G = nx.Graph()
```

```
# Add nodes for researchers and publications
G.add_node("AI in Healthcare")
G.add_node("Deep Learning for Medical Imaging")
G.add_node("John Doe (Researcher)")

# Create edges to show relationships between entities
G.add_edge("AI in Healthcare", "Deep Learning for Medical Imaging", weight=0.8)
G.add_edge("John Doe (Researcher)", "AI in Healthcare", weight=0.9)

# Visualize the graph (for simplicity, we use print)
for node in G.nodes
    print(f"Node {node}, Connected to {list(G.neighbors(node))}")
```

This graph structure can be extended to create a robust, scalable academic search system.

Search Using Natural Language Understanding (NLU)

In the legal domain, AI-powered search engines are increasingly important for assisting lawyers, legal researchers, and individuals in navigating legal texts such as statutes, case law, and legal briefs. Traditional search engines struggle to deal with the nuances of legal language, where precision is crucial. AI, specifically **Natural Language Understanding (NLU)**, allows for better parsing and interpretation of complex legal texts, making it easier to retrieve relevant legal information.

Legal search engines using NLU can identify the intent of a user's query, even when the query is not an exact match for the text in legal documents. For example, a user might search for "requirements for a valid contract," and an AI-powered search engine would identify terms like "contract," "requirements," and "validity," and return relevant case law or statutes related to contract formation.

Case-based reasoning is another technique in legal search engines, where AI systems recommend legal cases or statutes that are similar to the current case based on historical data. **Text classification** techniques can be employed to classify legal documents into categories such as case law, statutes, legal opinions, or regulations.

Example using **spaCy** for legal NLU

```
import spacy

# Load a legal NLU model (a custom legal NLP model)
nlp = spacy.load('en_core_web_sm')

# Sample legal query
text = "What are the requirements for a valid contract in California?"

# Process the query
doc = nlp(text)

# Extract relevant entities (e.g., 'valid contract', 'California')
```

```
for ent in doc.ents
    print(f"{ent.text} {ent.label_}")
```

This allows the search engine to detect specific legal terms and identify the best matches for the query.

AI-powered search engines have revolutionized the way specialized domains such as **e-commerce**, **medicine**, **academia**, and **law** access and process information. By leveraging advanced AI techniques like **personalized recommendations**, **entity recognition**, **citation analysis**, **natural language understanding**, and **knowledge graphs**, these search engines can provide highly relevant, accurate, and contextual results tailored to the needs of professionals and users within these domains. These innovations ensure that users can navigate vast, complex datasets more efficiently, empowering them to make better, informed decisions. Through continuous refinement and integration of AI technologies, the future of specialized domain search engines holds immense potential for improving accessibility and accuracy in these critical fields.

Chapter 14

Building a Search Engine from Scratch – A Complete Project

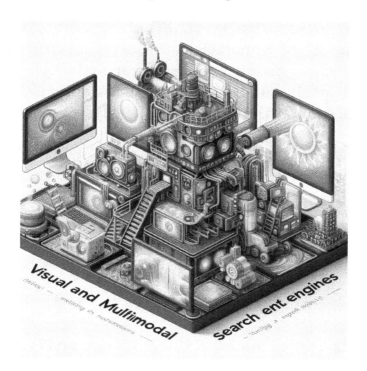

Creating an AI-powered search engine from scratch is a complex yet rewarding endeavor. Modern search engines go beyond simple keyword matching, incorporating natural language processing (NLP), machine learning-based ranking models, and scalable backend architectures to deliver fast and accurate search results. This chapter provides a detailed, step-by-step guide to building a fully functional search engine using **Django or Flask** for the backend, integrating **NLP models** for query understanding, implementing **machine learning models** for ranking search results, and deploying the system on **AWS or Google Cloud Platform (GCP)**.

By following this project, readers will gain hands-on experience in developing a sophisticated search system from the ground up, covering all key components, including data indexing, query processing, ranking optimization, and cloud deployment. The project will include full **code examples**, sample configurations, and deployment instructions to ensure a comprehensive learning experience.

Setting Up the Backend Using Django or Flask

To build a search engine, we need a robust backend to handle user queries, retrieve relevant documents, and return ranked results. We can use **Django** or **Flask**, two popular Python web frameworks, to build this backend.

Django is a high-level web framework that provides built-in tools for managing databases, authentication, and APIs. **Flask**, on the other hand, is a lightweight framework that gives developers more flexibility in designing their architecture.

For our implementation, we will use **Flask** because of its simplicity and minimal overhead.

Installing Flask and Setting Up the Project

First, install Flask and the required dependencies

```
pip install flask flask-restful elasticsearch
```

Next, create a **Flask app** for handling search queries.

```
from flask import Flask, request, jsonify
from elasticsearch import Elasticsearch

app = Flask(__name__)
es = Elasticsearch("http //localhost 9200")   # Connecting to Elasticsearch

@app.route('/search', methods=['GET'])
def search()
    query = request.args.get('query')
    response = es.search(index="documents", body={
      "query" {
```

```
        "match" {
            "content"  query
        }
    }
})
    return jsonify(response["hits"]["hits"])

if __name__ == '__main__'
    app.run(debug=True)
```

This simple Flask API takes a **query** as input, searches an Elasticsearch index, and returns relevant documents.

To run the Flask app

```
python app.py
```

Now, the backend is ready to receive and process user queries.

Integrating an NLP Model for Query Understanding

Search engines today rely on **NLP models** to understand queries beyond simple keyword matching. **Transformer-based models** like **BERT (Bidirectional Encoder Representations from Transformers)** and **Sentence Transformers** enable **semantic search**, allowing the engine to understand the intent behind user queries.

144

To implement NLP-based query processing, we will use **Sentence Transformers** to convert search queries and documents into vector representations. This allows the search engine to retrieve results based on semantic similarity.

Installing and Using Sentence Transformers

First, install the required library

pip install sentence-transformers

Now, load the **BERT-based Sentence Transformer** model and convert text into **vectors**

```
from sentence_transformers import SentenceTransformer
import numpy as np

# Load pre-trained sentence transformer model
model = SentenceTransformer('all-MiniLM-L6-v2')

# Convert search query into vector representation
query = "Latest research on AI in healthcare"
query_embedding = model.encode(query)

print(query_embedding.shape)  # Output (384,)
```

Each **query** is transformed into a **vector**, which allows us to perform **vector search** instead of simple text matching.

Using FAISS for Fast Vector Search

We can store document embeddings in **FAISS (Facebook AI Similarity Search)** for fast retrieval.

pip install faiss-cpu

Store and retrieve document embeddings

```
import faiss

# Initialize FAISS index
dimension = 384  # Embedding size from MiniLM model
index = faiss.IndexFlatL2(dimension)

# Add document embeddings (Example  3 document vectors)
document_embeddings        =         np.random.rand(3,
dimension).astype('float32')
index.add(document_embeddings)

# Search using query embedding
k = 2  # Retrieve top 2 most similar results
distances, indices = index.search(query_embedding.reshape(1, -
1), k)

print("Most relevant documents ", indices)
```

This method enables **real-time semantic search**, providing **context-aware** results rather than just keyword-based results.

Implementing a Machine Learning Model for Ranking

To improve search accuracy, we need a **ranking model** that orders search results based on relevance. A **Learning to Rank (LTR)** model can be used to score documents based on multiple factors like **query-document similarity, click-through rates, and user engagement**.

A simple approach is to use **XGBoost** for training a ranking model

Installing and Using XGBoost

pip install xgboost

Train an XGBoost model using search logs

```
import xgboost as xgb
import numpy as np

# Sample training data (features   query-document similarity,
CTR, etc.)
X_train = np.array([[0.8, 5], [0.6, 3], [0.4, 1]])
y_train = np.array([1, 0, 0])  # Labels (1  relevant, 0  not relevant)

# Train ranking model
model     =     xgb.XGBRanker(objective='rank     pairwise',
booster='gbtree', eta=0.1, max_depth=3)
model.fit(X_train, y_train)
```

```
# Predict ranking scores for new queries
X_test = np.array([[0.7, 4], [0.5, 2]])
rank_scores = model.predict(X_test)

print("Rank scores ", rank_scores)
```

This model helps re-rank search results to improve **user experience and relevance**.

Deploying the Search Engine on AWS or GCP

After building the search engine, we need to deploy it so that users can access it in **real-time**. We can use **AWS (Amazon Web Services) or GCP (Google Cloud Platform)** for deployment.

Deploying with Docker and Kubernetes

To deploy the Flask API, we containerize it using **Docker**

```
# Dockerfile
FROM python 3.9

WORKDIR /app

COPY requirements.txt .
RUN pip install -r requirements.txt

COPY . .
```

```
CMD ["python", "app.py"]
```

Build and run the Docker container

```
docker build -t search-engine .
docker run -p 5000 5000 search-engine
```

For **scalability**, we deploy on **Kubernetes**

```
# kubernetes-deployment.yaml
apiVersion  apps/v1
kind  Deployment
metadata
  name  search-engine
spec
  replicas  3
  selector
   matchLabels
     app  search-engine
  template
   metadata
    labels
      app  search-engine
   spec
    containers
    - name  search-engine
      image  search-engine latest
      ports
      - containerPort  5000
```

Deploy on **AWS/GCP Kubernetes Cluster**

```
kubectl apply -f kubernetes-deployment.yaml
```

In this chapter, we built a **complete AI-powered search engine** from scratch, covering all critical components setting up a **Flask backend**, integrating an **NLP model** for **semantic search**, implementing **learning-to-rank models**, and **deploying** the search engine on **AWS/GCP**. This hands-on project provides readers with a comprehensive understanding of modern search engine architecture, empowering them to build **custom AI-driven search solutions** for real-world applications.

Chapter 15

Future Trends in AI-Powered Search

The evolution of search technology has been rapid, and with the integration of artificial intelligence, the future promises even more transformative advancements. As we look ahead, search engines will continue to evolve beyond traditional keyword-based retrieval and embrace cutting-edge technologies such as **federated learning, quantum computing, multimodal search with AR/VR, and AI-generated search summaries**. These advancements will enhance the **speed, accuracy, personalization, and interactivity** of search experiences, making search engines more **context-aware, privacy-focused, and efficient**.

This chapter will explore the most promising future trends in AI-powered search, delving into how these technologies will shape the way people access, interact with, and interpret information.

Learning and Decentralized Search Engines

One of the major concerns in search engine technology today is **data privacy**. Traditional search engines rely on centralized models, meaning user data is stored in large-scale **data centers**, leading to privacy risks, security concerns, and monopolization of information retrieval. **Federated learning** is emerging as a viable solution to this challenge.

Federated learning is a **machine learning approach** that enables AI models to be trained across multiple devices without transferring raw data to a central server. Instead of sending personal data to a cloud server for analysis, each device processes search queries locally and only transmits **model updates** to a global AI model.

For instance, in a federated learning search engine, a user's device can process search queries, learn from interactions, and improve local ranking algorithms without sharing personal search histories. A **decentralized search engine** powered by **blockchain technology** and **federated learning** ensures that user data remains private while still benefiting from AI-driven search improvements.

Comparison Centralized vs. Federated Search

Feature	Centralized Search Engines	Federated Search Engines
Data Storage	Stored on central servers	Stored on user devices
Privacy Risk	High	Low
Personalization	Based on cloud-	Based on local device

Feature	Centralized Search Engines	Federated Search Engines
	stored profiles	learning
Computational Load	Heavy server-side processing	Distributed processing across devices

The transition toward federated learning and decentralized search engines could redefine how users interact with AI-powered search systems, offering **enhanced privacy** while maintaining efficiency.

Quantum Computing for Faster Search Processing

As the **volume of data** on the internet grows exponentially, conventional computing methods struggle to process complex search queries in real-time. **Quantum computing** is expected to revolutionize search engine technology by significantly **accelerating search processing speeds** and **enhancing AI-driven ranking algorithms**.

How Quantum Computing for Search Engines

Superposition for Simultaneous Processing
Unlike classical computers, which process data in

binary (0s and 1s), quantum computers leverage **qubits**, which can exist in **multiple states simultaneously**. This allows search engines to evaluate millions of search results at once, drastically reducing latency.

Quantum Machine Learning for Improved Ranking
Quantum-enhanced AI models can **analyze vast datasets** more efficiently than traditional models, leading to **better ranking predictions** and **more accurate personalized recommendations**.

Optimization of Search Algorithms
Quantum algorithms such as **Grover's algorithm** can improve search efficiency by **reducing the number of operations required** to find relevant information.

Traditional vs. Quantum Search Processing

Feature	Traditional Computing	Quantum Computing
Processing Speed	Linear Search	Parallel Search
Data Handling	Limited by hardware	Exponential scalability
Search Latency	Higher with large datasets	Near-instantaneous

Feature	Traditional Computing	Quantum Computing
AI Model Training	Time-intensive	Optimized for faster learning

Quantum computing remains in its early stages, but as the technology matures, search engines will **evolve from text-based retrieval systems into highly intelligent knowledge processors** capable of handling **vast, interconnected datasets in real-time**.

Multimodal Search Engines with AR/VR Interfaces

Search engines are moving beyond text-based queries and embracing **multimodal interactions**, where users can search using **voice, images, gestures, and even augmented or virtual reality (AR/VR) interfaces**. The combination of **computer vision, natural language processing, and AI-driven intent analysis** is making search experiences more intuitive and immersive.

Key Advancements in Multimodal Search

Visual Search with Augmented Reality (AR)
AI-powered visual search engines allow users to **point their smartphone camera** at an object to retrieve

information. For example, Google Lens enables users to **identify products, landmarks, or even plants and animals** instantly.

Voice-Activated Search and Conversational AI AI-driven assistants like **Google Assistant, Siri, and Alexa** are making voice search a standard mode of interaction. Future advancements in **speech recognition and intent detection** will enable users to have **conversational, context-aware interactions with search engines**.

VR-Based Search Experiences Imagine a **virtual library** where users can **browse, interact, and explore information** using a VR headset. AI-driven search engines could revolutionize **education, gaming, e-commerce, and medical research** by offering fully immersive search environments.

Multimodal Search Interaction Model

Below is a diagram showcasing the interaction between different input modes in a multimodal search engine.

The growing adoption of **multimodal search** will redefine user engagement, making search engines **more interactive, accessible, and natural**.

AI-Generated Search Summaries

The future of search will not only focus on **retrieving** information but also on **generating meaningful insights** for users. AI-powered **summarization models** like **GPT-4, BERTSUM, and T5** are transforming how users consume search results.

Instead of displaying **multiple links**, AI-driven search engines will **summarize** the most relevant information in a structured format. This technology is already visible in **Google's "Featured Snippets"** and AI-generated responses in search assistants.

How AI-Generated Summaries Will Change Search

Faster Information Retrieval
Users will no longer need to **click through multiple pages** to gather relevant data; instead, AI models will **synthesize key points** in real-time.

Context-Aware Insights
AI models can **analyze the user's search history, intent, and context** to generate **personalized responses**.

Multi-Source Content Aggregation
Future search engines may combine **news, research**

papers, and social media discussions into a **single AI-generated summary**, offering **holistic insights**.

Example Traditional vs. AI-Powered Search Results

Search Query	Traditional Search	AI-Generated Summary
"Latest AI advancements in healthcare"	Multiple links to research papers, blogs, and news articles	A concise summary combining key points from research papers, blogs, and expert opinions

This shift toward **AI-generated search responses** will **enhance user experience, reduce information overload, and improve search accuracy**.

AI-powered search engines are poised for groundbreaking advancements, **integrating** *federated learning for privacy, quantum computing for efficiency, multimodal interfaces for interaction, and AI-driven summaries for faster information retrieval.* **As these technologies evolve, search engines will transition from** *passive information retrieval tools* **to** *intelligent knowledge assistants* **capable of** *understanding, predicting, and contextualizing user intent* **like never before. By staying ahead of these trends, researchers, developers, and businesses can leverage AI to build** *next-generation search engines* **that redefine how information is accessed and consumed in the digital age.**

THE END

www.ingramcontent.com/pod-product-compliance
Lightning Source LLC
Chambersburg PA
CBHW070959050326
40689CB00014B/3422